ON YOUR OWN
as a YOUNG ADULT

Self-Advocacy Case Studies

BETSY KREBS
PAUL PITCOFF

On Your Own as a Young Adult: Self-Advocacy Case Studies

© 2006 by Betsy Krebs and Paul Pitcoff

Published by JIST Life, an imprint of JIST Publishing, Inc.

8902 Otis Avenue

Indianapolis, IN 46216-1033

Phone: 1-800-648-JIST   Fax: 1-800-JIST-FAX

E-mail: info@jist.com   Web site: www.jist.com

Support material available for this book includes *On Your Own as a Young Adult Facilitator's Guide* (1-55864-165-3) and the video *On Your Own as a Young Adult* (DVD 1-55864-167-X and VHS 1-55864-166-1).

Visit www.jist.com for information on JIST, free job search information, book excerpts, and ordering information on our many products! For free information on 14,000 job titles, visit www.careeroink.com

Quantity discounts are available for JIST books. Please call our Sales Department at 1-800-648-5478 for a free catalog and more information.

Acquisitions Editors: Barb Terry and Randy Haubner
Development Editor: Jill Mazurczyk
Cover Designer: designLab
Interior Designer: Aleata Howard
Interior Layout: Marie Kristine Parial-Leonardo
Proofreader: Linda Quigley

Printed in the United States
10 09 08 07 06 05   9 8 7 6 5 4 3 2 1

We have been careful to provide accurate information in this book, but it is possible that errors and omissions have been introduced. Please consider this in making any career plans or other important decisions. Trust your own judgment above all else and in all things.

Trademarks: All brand names and product names used in this book are trade names, service marks, trademarks, or registered trademarks of their respective owners.

ISBN 1-55864-164-5

About This Book

On Your Own as a Young Adult: Self-Advocacy Case Studies will help you learn how to gain the support you need to achieve your goals and take control of your life.

You will learn how to become a self-advocate by studying real cases about young people who have handled challenges in their lives. By studying and analyzing their cases, you can better prepare for your own future.

By studying these cases you will learn

- How to plan and reach your goals
- How systems and organizations work
- How your strengths are important
- How to make transitions
- How to find mentors and allies
- How to depersonalize issues
- How to recognize the needs of others
- How to use rules, laws, and rights
- How to make a self-advocacy presentation

After completing this book, you will be well on your way to becoming an independent self-advocate. Good luck!

Acknowledgments

We worked for many years developing *On Your Own as a Young Adult: Self-Advocacy Case Studies,* with the contributions of so many individuals, that we cannot thank all of them here. This book is the result of collaboration with young people from New York City, between the ages of 16 to 21, who, through enrolling in Youth Advocacy Center's seminars, were beginning the process of taking control of their futures. These young people provided us with thoughtful feedback, encouragement, and insight into how to make this book relevant and useful. In addition, they generously shared their experiences and stories, many of which are the basis for the cases here. We are deeply grateful to all these young people, for without their input, this book would never have been possible.

Youth Advocacy Center's former Program Director, Leigh Singer, is an outstanding teacher who taught many seminars using *On Your Own as a Young Adult.* She, along with other teachers of *On Your Own,* provided invaluable feedback and advice. Ashley Terletzky, Rebecca Iwerks, and Johanna Osburn helped make the text clearer and more useful for young people.

Many generous individuals, corporations, and foundations contributed financially to this project over the years, with major financial support from the Andrus Family Fund, the Annie E. Casey Foundation, the Bodman Foundation, the Catalog for Giving of New York, Hyde & Watson, JP Morgan/Chase, the Knossos Foundation, New Yorkers For Children, and the Open Society Institute. Youth Advocacy Center's Board of Directors also provided support for this project.

JIST Publishing's conviction that young people across the country should benefit from *On Your Own's* self-advocacy cases has been of singular importance for completing this project. In particular, we thank Barb Terry and Jill Mazurczyk for their enthusiasm, sensitivity, and attentiveness.

Finally, we appreciate the encouragement from our families, especially Harriet, Winton, and Noah Pitcoff; Lisa Ranghelli, George Pitt, Sheldon, Gabriel, and Daisy Stein; Ruth Pearl; and Jeffrey Krebs, for this project would not have been possible without their support.

If you would like training or more information about self-advocacy, informational interviews, or other topics in this book, please contact:

Youth Advocacy Center
281 Sixth Avenue
New York, NY 10014
Phone: 212-675-6181
Fax: 212-675-5724
www.youthadvocacycenter.org

Table of Contents

Introduction

We wrote *On Your Own as a Young Adult: Self-Advocacy Case Studies* for young adults like you who have dreams and goals for the future, but don't know exactly how to get there.

Our background is in law and education. We met when we worked together as lawyers representing children and young adults in court. We saw these young people needed more help to succeed in life, and so we started the Youth Advocacy Center in New York City to teach young adults how to reach their goals, handle challenges along the way, and start building a network for themselves through education and career planning. Young adults learn this by taking our Getting Beyond the System®: Self-Advocacy Seminar. *On Your Own as a Young Adult: Self-Advocacy Case Studies* is the book we use to teach the seminar. It has been tested for many years with young adults.

Most of the young adults we have worked with have used our seminar to begin serious thinking and planning for their future careers. They recognized that preparing for their future is important to reach successful independence and reach their life goals. We are proud and impressed that these young adults have used their intelligence and strengths, along with the Youth Advocacy Center's Getting Beyond the System Seminar, to overcome many hurdles and succeed in life.

These are some of the terms you will learn about in *On Your Own*.

- **Self-Advocacy**

  Self-advocacy is a way to empower yourself to reach your goals. Self-advocacy is a method to gain the support you need to achieve your goals. It's a process that requires you to learn to identify facts of a situation, analyze these facts (find out what the facts tell you), develop a convincing presentation to someone in a position to help you, and finally, to make a convincing presentation to that person. Self-advocacy derives from a legal model of thinking about negotiation. All successful people are good at self-advocacy. It is a skill you will use for your entire life.

- **The Case Method**

  This book is mainly a collection of *cases,* or stories, of young adults who have handled challenges in their lives. We have used these cases with hundreds of young adults before we published them here. We decided to teach self-advocacy using the Case Method (this is how most law schools teach future lawyers) because of the legal basis of self-advocacy and because we are impressed with the intellectual abilities of the young adults we have met. The Case Method requires you to read and think about the cases, answer questions, and then discuss them in class. Through this process, you will begin to learn the elements of self-advocacy and gain the ability to critically analyze facts.

- **The Socratic Approach**

  This seminar is designed around the Socratic approach to learning. Socrates was a philosopher in ancient Greece who believed that all people are smart enough to gain understanding by learning for themselves rather than being told what to do.

  Socrates was particularly respected and liked by the youth of Athens because he respected their thinking and was continually open to their ideas. Socrates worked hard to teach the youth how to think for themselves and not adopt ideas unless they themselves believed in them. His approach to teaching, especially when applied with youth, was not accepted by most of the adults in Athens; however, Socrates would not give up his approach nor his belief in the youth to become intellectually independent. In this book, we use the same approach Socrates used more than 2,000 years ago. It is an approach used in almost every law school and many other schools throughout the United States.

  In adopting the Socratic approach, we designed this case study book around the idea that you must be fully empowered to make your own decisions in life and that facilitators must respect those decisions. It is the facilitator's job to help you get as much information as possible and learn how to analyze that information. But in the end, empowerment means you set your own goals and plan your own path to reach those goals.

  You can do it!

In any new learning process, whether going to law school, taking a vocational training course, learning to teach, or learning how to cook, most people at first feel overwhelmed. They often think there is too much to learn, the method of learning seems strange, or it's going too fast and demanding too much time. These reactions are normal. Successful people just recognize that if they stay with the learning long enough, it will become easier and worthwhile.

The work you will have to do using *On Your Own* is challenging, but it is also enjoyable. At first, most users find the method, the reading, and the questions difficult. As you become familiar with the method, the cases and questions will get easier. We know you are smart and can do the work, and we respect this fact by providing you with a challenging and important learning experience.

Betsy Krebs
Executive Director
Youth Advocacy Center, Inc.
New York, New York

Paul Pitcoff
Director of Education
Youth Advocacy Center, Inc.
New York, New York

The Self-Advocacy Process

If you master the self-advocacy process, you will have great success in reaching your goals throughout your life. During this seminar, you will learn the following skills that will make you a successful self-advocate:

- Set **goals.**

- Make **plans** for how to reach your goals.

- Develop a plan based on an understanding of how **organizations work.**

- Identify **personal strengths** that will demonstrate likelihood of success.

- Use the advice and support of **mentors and allies.**

- Analyze the **needs** of the "other person" and **depersonalize** the issues.

- Develop and communicate **workable solutions.**

- Develop a compelling self-advocacy presentation through designing an effective **agenda.**

- Conduct an **informational interview.**

- Use **rules and laws,** if necessary, to support your positions.

This is a lot to learn, but you can do it. Many young adults have taken the Youth Advocacy Center's seminar and used self-advocacy to successfully reach their goals. If you want control of your life, self-advocacy is an essential skill.

The Informational Interview

If you are studying self-advocacy, you are one of many students who want to take control of their lives and especially their future. An extremely useful means for getting information about your future career goals is to conduct an informational interview with someone who is successful in your chosen career field.

An informational interview is a meeting with an experienced professional in a career field you might be interested in as a long-term goal. The informational interview is an opportunity to get information about a specific job and what education, training, and experience are needed to get such a job. It is not a job interview. These types of interviews are very important. They can help you reach your goals much faster by learning the best ways to pursue your goals and making connections with people who can help you.

The informational interview will save you a great amount of time and make reaching your goals somewhat easier; therefore, it is extremely important. A skilled self-advocate depends upon good information, and informational interviews are an effective means to get particularly useful information. Most students find their informational interviews one of the most important experiences for moving ahead with their future as well as a way of practicing the self-advocacy skills they learned during the seminar.

Method for Briefing a Case

In *On Your Own as a Young Adult: Self-Advocacy Case Studies,* one of the main ways you will learn self-advocacy is by reading and analyzing situations. We call these situations "cases" and the process of analyzing them "briefing the case." This is what law students and lawyers do when they get a new case. The cases you will read are based on true stories of young adults who faced difficult challenges; they are situations you might encounter in the future.

When you are assigned a case, you must read it and answer questions about it:

- First, **read** the entire case through to get an overall understanding of the story.

- Second, **review** all the questions you must answer to brief the case.

- Third, **re-read** the entire case to discover your answers for each question.

- While reading the story a second time,

  - Underline important facts.

  - Write **G** in the margin next to the main character's **goals.**

  - Write **N** in the margin next to **needs** of the other people in the case.

  - Write **S** in the margin next to **strengths** of the main character (the person who the case is about).

  - Write **P/C** in the margin next to **primary challenge** the main character faces.

In each case, the main character has to deal with and work out a significant challenge, problem, or roadblock that is preventing him or her from reaching his or her goal. Only by identifying this **primary challenge** can a self-advocate develop a strategy for overcoming this challenge.

For most cases, you have to answer the following questions:

1. What are the important facts that relate to the primary challenge of the case?

   a. List the main character's **long- and short-term goals.**

b. Identify the **needs** of the person in a position to help the main character.

c. Describe the **strengths** of the main character.

d. Identify **missing information** that would be helpful in planning strategies.

2. What is the **primary challenge** that must be resolved (worked out) for the main character to reach his or her long- or short-term goals?

3. What kind of **general plan** would resolve (work out) the challenge you described above and move toward the main character's long-term goal?

Write your answers clearly, and when possible, use an outline format.

The goals of briefing a case or analyzing a real-life situation for self-advocacy purposes are to

- Fully understand and define **goals**

- Fully **understand** all the **reasons and motivations** the **"other person"** might have to support you in your efforts to achieve a goal

- Develop a presentation that will **convince** other people to support reaching your goals

Finally, to be an effective self-advocate, you need to develop the ability to be *specific* about facts and setting your goals. The more specific you are, the greater the chance the other person will understand you. For example, if you tell someone you don't need much money to live on, what does "much money" mean? To a rap star, that might be a million dollars or more a year; to a teacher, that might mean $40,000 a year; to a homeless person, that might mean $10,000 a year. The term "much money" is general, not specific.

Another example of being specific is when someone asks you about your strengths. If you respond by saying you are "responsible," that is a general and not a specific response. It might be better to explain how you were responsible for your sister when she came home from school, or that you voluntarily took the *Getting Beyond the System: Self-Advocacy*

Seminar, a challenging program that requires homework and full atten-
dance in order to help you reach the long-term goals you have established for yourself.

In your effort to be specific, you must ask yourself, "What do I mean by
using this word? Will other people know what I mean? Is there a better
description to make sure that the other person understands what I
mean?"

See Appendix B for an example of briefing a case.

CHAPTER 1

Planning for and Reaching Your Goals

Background

All-important to successful self-advocacy is good planning. Most activities involve planning. You often engage in planning without even thinking about the process. For example, you may plan

- A trip
- Shopping
- A strategy in sports
- How to cook a meal
- A party
- A day's schedule

The first step in planning is to identify your **goals** in an accurate, specific, and complete way. Every successful advocate—whether a lawyer trying a case, a businessperson negotiating a contract, or a tenant requesting repair of a broken refrigerator—understands the importance of setting goals. Goals can be long-term (they won't be reached for years) or short-term (they will be reached within a year). Once you set goals, you can then make plans to reach them.

To advocate for yourself, you must learn to set accurate and specific goals and develop a plan to reach them. This may be a new way of thinking and will take practice. The more skill you develop in setting your goals, the better your chances are of reaching them.

Example

Sabena is entering her senior year in high school. Her goal is to work as a radiology technologist. She knows she can earn around $38,000 per year after her training and several years of work experience. This is a good time for Sabena to begin to plan how to reach her goal. She needs to find out what education she will need, how she can finance or borrow money for her education and living expenses while she is in college, and what she needs to do to be accepted into a qualified education program. If she makes these plans now, Sabena will not waste any time after she graduates high school and will make good decisions in selecting the best path to becoming a radiology technologist.

Reaching long-term career and personal goals takes time, and you should begin the process now. Merely having an idea for a goal is not enough. You must get information about your goals in order to make your goals accurate, specific, and comprehensive (complete). Having specific goals will help you make good plans to reach them.

To reach your goals, you will need to get other people to support your efforts. Whether it's a boss, a teacher, an advisor, someone who knows someone who can help you, or a work colleague, getting this "other person" to support your efforts is a major part of being successful. Using self-advocacy is a way to get others to support your efforts in achieving your goals. Thus, it is an important skill to learn.

The first step in self-advocacy is to set specific goals. The **benefits** of setting specific, accurate, and comprehensive goals and establishing plans to reach those goals are to

- Sharpen your knowledge and thinking about your goals
- Help make a realistic evaluation of the challenges you will need to prepare for
- Help you set priorities (what actions are most important)
- Help maintain your focus on your goals
- Help you to manage a situation rather than just react emotionally
- Guide you through effective self-advocacy

Case #1:

Importance of Establishing Goals

Choosing career or professional goals is not easy. Starting to think about career goals is one way to take the first steps to becoming an advocate for yourself. It is critical in setting goals that you have enough information about the benefits and challenges of the goals you select.

Shavone's Five Career Choices

Shavone is 19 years old. She graduated high school last June with a "B" average. She lives with her aunt in kinship foster care and six younger cousins on Marcy Place, off the Grand Concourse in the Bronx. Her mother is very ill and her father has moved to Louisiana. Shavone's aunt has told Shavone that she must move out in a year.

Some of Shavone's older friends made the mistake of not thinking about their futures and not planning ahead. Many are struggling and have no idea of what they want for their futures. Shavone is determined that she will be successful and knows she must begin setting her long-term goals now.

Shavone wants and needs to be independent. Korin, her older sister, is a supervisor at a telephone company. Korin can help Shavone get a job as a data processing clerk at the phone company. The phone company offers some job security and opportunities for advancement.

Shavone has also thought about travel. She knows that if she works for an airline, she can get reduced prices on travel. She likes the idea of travel. She has thought of working as a flight attendant (takes care of passengers' safety and comfort on the plane) or as a pre-flight specialist (checks whether planes are ready for flight). She has also thought of becoming a flight controller (coordinates flights, landings, and takeoffs of airplanes from airports) working for the Federal Aviation Administration.

In thinking about her future, Shavone has thought about college. She wants her own children to have more advantages than she had and believes a college education will help her in raising and educating her own children. She has been told that college will help her get better jobs.

(continued)

(continued)

Shavone has also thought about a career in marketing. Marketing involves planning ways for a company to sell its products and services to customers. Planning how to advertise, how to package a product, where to sell it, and why people will find the products or services useful are all things a marketing professional does.

Finally, Shavone has often been complimented on how she dresses. Friends have urged her to open her own dress or clothing store. She likes this idea but knows nothing about running her own business.

Shavone recognizes that she must make decisions now about what she will do when she can no longer live with her aunt. If she sets goals now, she can begin to make useful plans to achieve her long-term goals. If she doesn't make good plans now, she may become so overwhelmed with the work of being independent that she will have no chance of reaching any of her goals. In spite of this, Shavone is not certain about which direction she should take.

Questions

1. What are the important facts that relate to the primary challenge of the case?

    a. List Shavone's **long- and short-term goals.**

    b. Describe Shavone's **strengths.**

    c. Identify **missing information** that would be helpful for Shavone in deciding which career goal to pursue.

2. What is the **primary challenge** (significant challenge, problem, or roadblock that is preventing someone from reaching his or her goal) that must be resolved for Shavone to reach her long- or short-term goals?

3. If you were Shavone, which of her four choices for a career would you select? Explain why you made this selection.

4. Does Shavone's background affect what career she pursues? Explain your answer.

5. What problems may Shavone encounter in pursuing the career goal you selected?

6. Why is it important that Shavone make up her mind now?

7. What are at least four actions Shavone should consider doing now in order to establish (set up) a long-term career goal? Describe these actions.

8. Does Shavone need to consider a college education? Why?

9. After Shavone moves out of her aunt's apartment, she will be completely responsible for herself. If she were to pursue Korin's job offer, Shavone could be comfortably independent. What are some compelling (important, key) reasons she should not accept this job at the phone company? How might Shavone turn the phone company job into something more to her liking? How do you weigh the short-term benefits of a choice with the possible long-term costs?

10. Think about your own career goals. What are two possible careers that you would like to be pursuing in five years from now? Give thought to your choices. For each selected career/profession,

   a. Explain what the profession is to someone who has no knowledge of it.

   b. Explain the personal benefits and problems with each selected profession.

   c. Explain what type of experience you need to have for each career you selected.

   d. Explain what type of education or training you need for each of your selected careers.

   e. Explain what you don't know about each of your selected careers and how you will get the information that you need.

   f. Explain the very next step you should take for each of your selected career goals.

Case #2:

Importance of Planning to Reach Goals

Everyone has to prepare for many job interviews in their lives. When you are starting out, you have little experience with job interviews and you—like everyone else—will make mistakes. If you can learn from your mistakes and from others, you will get much better at job interviews. One goal is to learn how to prepare for a job interview and learn how to correct mistakes.

Background: What Is a Mutual Fund?

A *mutual fund* combines the money that many different individuals have saved and "invests" it in different corporations.

Investing consists of buying a small share of a corporation. If the corporation does well, this share can be sold for more money. If the corporation does poorly, the investor can lose all of his or her invested money. Investing has risks but it can help a person make more money from money he or she has saved.

- For example: Brian is a pastry chef. He wants to save money for his child's education and to continue his college education. He has saved $3,000 over 13 months of work and is thinking about moving it from his bank to a mutual fund. If the money is invested in good companies, Brian might expect to get almost 6% to 8% a year ($180–$240). There is a chance that Brian could lose his entire investment ($3,000) but the mutual fund has a good reputation for selecting solid companies. If Brian puts his money in a bank, he would get approximately 1.25% a year ($37.50). However, the bank deposit is totally safe. He can never lose his money.

  Brian figures that investing will get him an extra $142.50 to $202.50 the first year and more than that the next year with "compounding." If he does not take out any money, and he averages 8% a year, in

  - 5 years his $3,000 would be worth as much as $4,408

- 10 years it would be worth as much as $6,477

- 15 years Brian's original investment of $3,000 might be worth $9,517

If he left his $3,000 in the bank at 1.25% interest, he would only have in

- 5 years, $3,192

- 10 years, $3,397

- 15 years, $3,614

Because Brian doesn't need the money for the next five years, and the mutual fund will give a much larger return, he decides to take the risk and invest in the mutual fund.

Ebony's First Job Interview

The Case

Ebony is 20 years old. She is a sophomore at Roxburry Community College near Boston. Last year Ebony graduated from high school and received a regular diploma and a certificate of achievement in math. In her first year as a freshman at college, she maintained a "B" average.

Ebony lives with her father on Manthome Road in West Roxburry. Ebony hardly ever sees her father who is often working two jobs just to make ends meet. Ebony works at a King Burger near her school to pay for her food, clothing, schoolbooks, and living expenses. She doesn't make enough to help her father with rent. He is often angry that she can't pay some of the rent. On a few occasions he was so angry he told her to leave.

Even in the past, things were often rocky for Ebony. When she began high school, she hung out with a troublemaking crowd and was suspended from school twice for starting fights and taking other people's money. Three times she was suspended for being high. However, since the end of her junior year in high school, Ebony has worked hard and stayed out of trouble. While she has very little money, Ebony is known for dressing well and spending very little for her clothes. She is determined to have her own family, make enough money to remain independent, and be able to spend time with her husband and children.

(continued)

(continued)

Ebony understands that in order to protect herself and her future children she needs to have a good career. She wants to do something that is both interesting and makes good money with benefits. Ebony has developed some interest in business but doesn't know enough about it.

Last summer Ebony worked as a receptionist for a large advertising agency. Her responsibility was to make sure that all people who called or arrived at the advertising agency got to talk with the right person and were made to feel that the agency cared about them. She did well but had to leave after 11 weeks because she could not work the 40 hours and stay in school.

Ebony wants a better part-time job than working at King Burger. She would like to do something where she might learn more about business. Because she does not pay rent, her financial needs are not too large. However, she promised her father that she would begin to help with the rent by next year. Ebony wants to use this time to learn more about business and perhaps develop contacts to get a good job during her last two years in college.

Brian, a pastry chef, is a friend of Ebony's. He has a friend that works at E.L. Jenkins, a mutual fund company. Brian's friend said that E.L. Jenkins hires young people and pays well. It sounds good. Brian suggests that Ebony call the personnel office and ask if she could be interviewed for an "entry-level job" or apply as an intern, which is unpaid, but may turn into a job after a couple of months.

The Interview

Ebony gets an interview with Ms. Ward in the human resources department (personnel or hiring department) of E.L. Jenkins, a large mutual fund company. The interview is scheduled for 8:30 a.m. Due to Ebony's unfamiliarity with the neighborhood, she reaches the office at 8:52 a.m.

Ms. Ward: "You are late and I don't have much time. I understand you would like an entry-level position with us."

Ebony: "Yes."

Ms. Ward: "Have you thought of what department you would like to work in?"

Ebony: "Any place would be fine."

Ms. Ward: "What are your plans for the future?"

Ebony: "I want to finish college."

Ms. Ward: "What are you studying?"

Ebony: "A little of everything."

Ms. Ward: "Do you know anything about E.L. Jenkins?"

Ebony: "No...well, you're a mutual bank."

Ms. Ward: Smiles warmly and gets up from her chair and walks toward the door. "Ebony, you have an impressive résumé, but I'm not sure that E.L. Jenkins has anything to offer you. Thank you for your interest."

Hint: The interview did not go well! But the mistakes made by Ebony could be corrected.

Questions

1. What are the important facts that relate to the primary challenge of the case?

   a. List Ebony's **long- and short-term goals.**

   b. Identify the **needs** of Ms. Ward and E.L. Jenkins.

   c. Describe Ebony's **strengths.**

   d. Identify **missing information** that would be helpful in planning a better approach for the job interview.

2. What is the **primary challenge** that must be resolved by Ebony to reach her immediate goal of getting an opportunity to work at E.L. Jenkins?

3. What could be a **general plan** to resolve the challenge you described above and move toward Ebony's immediate goals?

4. How could Ebony have found out more about E.L. Jenkins?

5. Should it matter that Ebony was late if it wasn't her fault? Why? How could she have made sure she wouldn't be late?

6. Why is Ebony well suited for an internship at E.L. Jenkins?

7. How did Ebony communicate her suitability?

8. What could Ebony have done to improve her ability to communicate her strengths?

9. Does Ms. Ward like Ebony? How do you know? Does it matter?

Case #3

Making Specific Plans to Reach Goals

A strategy is a more careful and specific plan of action. Making a strategy helps you anticipate the range of challenges and be better prepared to reach your goals through self-advocacy.

Samantha's Strategy to Change Jobs at C&E Electronics

Samantha has been working at C&E Electronics on West Warren Avenue in Detroit for four months. C&E Electronics sells popular electronics and small appliances. They keep a good inventory (always supplied with popular brand-name items) and provide customers with good information about the products that they sell. C&E prices are often 5% to 10% above the biggest discount stores downtown. Samantha's job is to be on the floor and tell customers where different departments are in the store. Her salary is $6.21 an hour, and she does not get benefits. Samantha finds her job boring.

Samantha got this job because she is 18 years old and wants to move away from her parents and be independent. One of her goals is to have some money saved to help pay the first few months' rent and security deposit and to purchase some furniture when she moves into her own apartment. Samantha also wants to go to college and would like to have a steady job with convenient hours while she attends classes.

Samantha might like to become a business major and someday be a store manager. She has also been interested in studying psychology.

Now that Samantha has worked for four months, she thinks she would like to be in sales (working with customers). She knows a lot about the different television sets that are sold. She also thinks she would like to do some of the work related to ordering CDs, DVDs, or electronics. The one thing she knows is that she hates her present job and hates her supervisor.

Questions

1. What are the important facts that relate to the primary challenge of the case?

   a. List Samantha's **long- and short-term goals.**

b. Identify the **needs** of C&E Electronics.

c. Describe Samantha's **strengths.**

d. Identify **missing information** that would be helpful in planning strategies.

2. What is the **primary challenge** that must be resolved for Samantha to reach her short-term goal?

3. Samantha goes to her supervisor who is talking with another employee. Samantha tells the supervisor she hates her job and wants something better. Do you think this is a good approach? Why?

4. What should Samantha do *before* she talks to anyone about her desire to have a better job at C&E Electronics?

5. Plan a strategy for Samantha to approach C&E Electronics:

a. Who should she talk with?

b. How would she arrange this meeting?

c. What should she say?

Case #4

Using Fact Finding and Analysis to Set Goals

Decision-making—including establishing goals for your self-advocacy—requires good information and sharp analysis. The most effective self-advocates are highly skilled at seeking out good information and making insightful analysis (taking a number of complex facts and creating a simpler understanding) from that information.

Michael Needs to Find the Facts

Michael is 17 years old. He lives in a foster home in South Los Angeles. Since he was five years old, he has always wanted to own an automobile repair shop and someday an entire car dealership (sells and services automobiles). Michael has a six-month-old daughter with Sue. He plans to marry Sue in a year. Therefore, he needs to work at something that can support his daughter.

Michael has lived in three different foster homes over the past two-and-a-half years. Every six months he visits his Uncle Jordan who lives in San Diego. Jordan is the brake specialist at a large car dealership. Michael likes his uncle and almost went to live with him, but his uncle's house was not big enough.

Michael's high school experience has not been great. While he has done well in a science course, he has done poorly in most others. His teachers like him but are always telling him he has to work harder. Michael is popular with many friends and has a knack for staying out of serious trouble.

Last year a recruiter for one of the car companies visited Michael's high school. The recruiter offered a training program for high school graduates who want to learn car repair. After a two-month training, a person can get a beginning job as an apprentice mechanic for $9.35 an hour. Michael was interested, but the only openings were in cities in Florida and Arizona, and he really doesn't want to move away from Los Angeles.

Michael's Uncle Jordan told him that if he wants to run a car dealership, he should go to college and get it over with while he is young. "Why waste the benefits of a college education now, when it would help you the most?" was his uncle's advice.

Michael has to decide whether to take the mechanic's training, go to college, or do something else. He is so confused that he is not making any decision and is thinking that he'll just see how things turn out.

Hint: Michael needs to take more control of his future right now!

Questions

1. What are the important facts that relate to the primary challenge of the case?

    a. List Michael's **long- and short-term goals.**

    b. Identify the **needs** of Michael's uncle and the recruiter.

    c. Describe Michael's **strengths.**

    d. Identify **missing information** that would be helpful in planning strategies.

2. What is the **primary challenge** Michael must resolve to begin taking control of his future?

3. What should Michael consider in making a decision about what career path to pursue?

4. In order of importance, list good reasons for Michael to go to college now.

5. In order of importance, list good reasons for Michael to take the mechanic's training now.

6. What are the facts that demonstrate that Michael will have the ability to run a car dealership?

Exercise #1

Identifying Your Long- and Short-Term Goals

In order to get important information and begin planning for your future, it is useful to begin thinking of career and personal goals now. Write out your answers to the following questions. You may not know the answers to all the questions but do the best you can.

Questions

1. **Long-Term Goals**

   a. What type of job or career will you be working toward in five years?

   b. Where will you be living in five years?

   c. What will be the most important changes you will have to make in your life to reach these goals?

2. **Short-Term Goals**

   a. What things will you have to do to reach your career goals?

   b. What are your education goals?

   General   High School

   College

   Specific training (technical or trade school)

   Specific   What major will you select in college?

   What other training will you need?

   What books should you read?

   What specific skills do you need to learn?

What other sources of career information do you need to look at?

Who would you want to have informational interviews with?

c. What are your job and internship goals before you reach your five-year career goal?

General   Jobs to support yourself until you reach your long-term job objectives

Specific   Jobs/internships to gain experience and contacts for long-term job goals

Many individuals take jobs that are not this specific 5-year career goals, but are important steps to reaching their goals. For example, you many have to take a job to support yourself while you work toward your long-term career goals. Or you may take a job or internship to gain experience and contacts for your long-term job goals.

Think about this and try to identify short-term job and internship goals you might have before you reach your long-term career goal.

Example: "My long-term career goal is to sell advertising for a music magazine. I need to get a college education to learn about business and to improve my ability to understand and communicate with others. While I'm going to college, I want to work at a magazine, newspaper, or media company in their sales or advertising department to learn more about the business and earn enough money to support myself through college. While in college, I'll take any job, such as a receptionist, messenger, or clerk, at a magazine, newspaper, or media company just to be around people who work in the field and make contacts even if that job is not exactly what I want."

CHAPTER 2

How Systems and Organizations Work

Background

An *organization* is a group of people who have a common goal. Most self-advocacy involves getting the support of an organization. When you make your self-advocacy presentation to a person, she or he most likely represents an organization. You come into contact with organizations in every aspect of your daily life. The following are all examples of organizations:

- High School
- College
- Family
- Business
- Sports team
- Government
- Religious group
- Hospital

Successful self-advocates understand how organizations work. To advocate for yourself, you need to know the **organization's goals.** You also need to know **who has responsibility for specific activities**, who has the **power or authority in the organization to make decisions**, and who doesn't.

Usually, when you advocate for yourself, you are dealing with people (the "other person") who represent an organization, not just their own interests. Therefore, you must understand the organization's goals in order to get support for your goals. People will be motivated to help you if helping you supports the goals of their organizations.

The other person (usually representing an organization) is anyone that can help the self-advocate reach his or her personal goals.

- For a lawyer, the other person might be another attorney or the judge.

- For a nurse, the other person might be a supervisor, a doctor, a member of a patient's family, or a drug company.

- For a businessperson, the other person might be a client (individual or organization served by the businessperson), a vendor (individual or organization that sells goods or services to the businessperson), a manufacturer (individual or organization that makes things for the businessperson), or an investor (individual or organization that gives money for a portion of ownership).

- For a community activist, the other person might be a government official.

For you, the other person might be your employer, teacher, parent, foster parent, friend, caseworker, boss, coach, or landlord. While it is easy to think that your success in gaining the support of the other person depends on your personal relationship, you must always keep in mind that the other people also represent the needs and goals of their organizations. They will judge your request based upon how they think it will support their organizations' goals.

Some people resist (do not want to) thinking about the needs of others. It makes them feel inferior. Successful self-advocates accept these feelings but realize their primary focus is to reach their own goals. A good self-advocate recognizes that in order to reach his or her goals, he or she will most likely need to support some of the goals and needs of the others and the organizations they represent.

The following is a good example of making a proposal based on the goals of the organization.

Example

Chantel lives with a roommate in the Bronx. Since she graduated high school, she has worked for Springtime Gardening Service. Her job is to plant ornamental bushes in backyards and terraces throughout New York City. Chantel would like to be the person who goes to the plant nurseries (the places that grow the ornamental bushes) and selects and buys the ornamental bushes that Springtime plants for its customers.

Chantel recognizes that Springtime's goal is to make money by planting the most beautiful ornamental bushes. Most important to Springtime is that these bushes survive year after year and bring pleasure to their customers.

Chantel makes a proposal to the owner of Springtime with the following points:

- For more than two years I have planted ornamental bushes. From my experience, I know which bushes customers enjoy the most and which types of bushes grow well or didn't grow well.

- If I were made a "buyer" (responsible for selecting bushes), more customers would be satisfied and there would be less complaints about bushes that did not survive.

- More customer satisfaction and less complaints would add to Springtime's reputation and get more customers.

- Fewer bush replacements would save Springtime money.

- A promotion to buyer and an increase in my salary would be more than paid for by the additional income to Springtime from more satisfied customers and fewer bushes dying.

- I would be willing to train a new person on my time to take my job. This would not cost Springtime any money for hiring a replacement.

Notice how Chantel focused attention on the needs of the organization to advocate for a promotion.

Concepts to Consider When Working with These Cases

An organization

- Is an association of people connected to each other by a mission (a common goal).

- Usually has rules and agreed upon principles.

- Has people who fall into a hierarchy (order of importance) of responsibility, accountability, and power. The person who is completely in charge delegates (assigns, gives out) responsibility and authority to others for specific tasks. For example, the owner (person who is completely in charge) of a printing business will put someone in charge of the following divisions or areas in the business:

  - **Marketing:** attracting new clients and customers
  - **Sales:** finding and acquiring (getting) customers
  - **Account management:** keeping and servicing clients
  - **Production:** actual printing
  - **Buyer:** purchasing paper, ink, and supplies for printing
  - **Financial:** accounting, paying bills, and collecting fees

Organizations' Missions

All organizations have missions. A mission can be thought of as an organization's overall or long-term goal. Whether you want to get a job, join a group, or work with an organization, you need to understand the organization's mission.

Background

Jamal Finds the Missions

When Jamal was 19, he was all on his own, except for a friend who got him a night job at a large package delivery company in Houston, Texas. He quickly realized the work was hard and boring and not something he would want to do the rest of his life. He decided he would have to go to college in order to get a better education and the opportunity to get a more interesting job.

Going to college was very difficult for Jamal. He had to get financial aid, borrow money, and work part-time. The college work was much more difficult than high school. While he was in college, a number of his teachers commented on his ability to make people feel comfortable. A marketing teacher suggested he go into sales because he was good with people and was also very good at understanding other people's needs.

Jamal now works as a salesperson for Program Designs (PD), a computer programming company. (Computer programs are ways workers can use their computers to do important things for their business. For example, a computer program can plan the best route for a delivery truck making many deliveries.) PD designs custom software (computer programs) to help businesses save time and work more efficiently. Jamal's job is to sell PD's services to different organizations.

Jamal is lining up a number of businesses that might benefit from PD's custom software. His plan is to have two meetings with these potential clients (business customers). Jamal will call each business and ask whether he can meet with their top executives. At this first meeting, Jamal will find out about the **needs** of the business, what products they sell, how they sell these products, what they identify as their long-term goals, and whether they have any problems with running the business.

(continued)

(continued)

> Within two weeks after this first meeting, Jamal will follow up with a presentation of a plan for custom software that will help the company save time and money and increase efficiency in order to reach their long-term organizational goals. He will also explain PD's services and costs.
>
> Jamal knows that getting the first meeting to collect specific information is the hardest step. To get this meeting, he will have to demonstrate at least some overall understanding of the organization's needs and mission.

Example

Jamal thinks that R.B. Plumbing would benefit from PD's services. He knows that R.B. Plumbing offers free estimates (informing how much it will cost the customer) to customers considering plumbing jobs. This is a big advantage to customers because other plumbers charge by the hour plus materials and don't give any estimate of how much the job will cost. Thus, a customer might pay much more than he or she expected when the job is completed.

If PD can develop software that will reduce the time it takes to make estimates and make the estimates more accurate, it will save R.B. Plumbing time and money. Because Jamal knows that the main way R.B. gets customers is through free estimates, Jamal will call R.B. Plumbing and ask them if they would be interested in a service that would help them save time and be more accurate in making estimates. Jamal is confident that they will want the software he is selling. Jamal believes R.B. Plumbing will be interested in a meeting where Jamal can learn about R.B. Plumbing's specific needs and then present his solutions.

Question

The following is a list of the organizations Jamal intends to contact. For each one, he needs to understand the mission of the organization so he can offer valuable computer software. Try to analyze what you think is the mission for each of the following companies. All these organizations want to make a profit (money), but ask yourself, "How does each organization want to accomplish this goal? How does each one make their organization stand out and be different from the rest?"

- The PAG, a specialty clothing and accessory chain of stores
- Phil's Bakery, specializing in eight different types of bread and specialty muffins
- C&E Electronics, sells popular electronics and small appliances
- ENVY, a dance club
- Hannibal Bookstore specializing in self-help books

Case #5

Matching Your Goals with the Needs of an Organization

Often when you need something from an organization, you have to negotiate with a supervisor. This can be frustrating when that person seems to have a lot on his or her mind and doesn't really care about what you want or need. Trying to understand what that person is concerned about can help you reach your goals.

Nat Wants to Change His Lunch Hour at Baldwin's Hardware

Nat has been working as a stock clerk (places items for sale on shelves) at Baldwin's Hardware store for four months. Baldwin's is open Monday through Saturday between 8:00 a.m. and 5:00 p.m. On Thursday evenings, Baldwin's has special sales and instruction on tools from 7:00 p.m. to 8:30 p.m. Nat works from 8:00 a.m. to 5:00 p.m., Tuesday through Saturday. He normally gets off for lunch from 12:30 p.m. to 1:30 p.m.

Nat's friend Harnette is getting out of the hospital on Tuesday at 2:00 p.m. Harnette needs help getting home and Nat is the only one who can help him. Nat and Harnette have plans to open their own construction company, specializing in fixing and building cabinets, shelves, and storage spaces in people's apartments.

It is 8:51 a.m. on Tuesday, the day Harnette is coming home from the hospital. Alicia is working the cash register. Danielle, the store manager, hired Alicia seven months ago. Two months ago, Alicia was given the responsibility for scheduling all the employees as well as the tool instruction events on Thursday evenings.

Before work, Alicia's mother yelled at her for staying out late. Alicia wants to go to college, but she doesn't make enough money to pay for both school and for her own apartment. Three months ago, Alicia's boyfriend died in a car accident.

There is a morning rush of customers. It is a very hot summer day. Tanya has just returned a fan because the plug fell off. She doesn't want a replacement, just her money back. Tanya is agitated and accuses Alicia of selling "junk." Three other customers are waiting in line. They are impatient and angry because Alicia hasn't let them pay for their purchases.

Alicia does not know whether to give Tanya her money back. She decides to lock the cash register and go find Danielle in the back of the store. Danielle never seems pleased with Alicia's decisions, and therefore, Alicia does not want to make this decision on her own.

As Alicia walks back to find Danielle, she passes Nat who is restocking light bulbs. As Alicia passes Nat, he tells her about his needs. "Hey Alicia, you lookin' down!" Alicia barely pauses as she continues toward Danielle. Nat continues as Alicia walks away. "Anyway... I'm changing my lunch hour today. I have to take my friend..."

Nat doesn't get a chance to explain that his friend is coming home from the hospital and needs his help. Before reaching Danielle, Alicia denies Nat's request. "If you change your lunch time today, don't bother coming back...ever!" As Alicia gets to Danielle's office in the back, she turns toward Nat, "You think I look down—your face scares the dead!"

Nat is furious. He has worked at Baldwin's Hardware store for four months and has never asked to switch his lunch hour. If this is the way he is going to be treated, he will quit. He will leave at 1:30 p.m. and just never come back!

Questions

1. What are the important facts that relate to the primary challenge of the case?

   a. List Nat's **long- and short-term goals.**

   b. Identify Alicia's **needs.**

   c. Identify the needs of Baldwin's Hardware.

   d. Identify Danielle's needs.

   e. Describe Nat's **strengths.**

   f. Identify **missing information** that would be helpful in planning strategies.

2. What is the **primary challenge** that Nat must resolve to reach his immediate goal?

3. What are specific reasons why Alicia does not help Nat?

4. Are there any other ways Nat could have handled this situation?

   a. Describe how Nat could have approached this situation in a better way before he saw Alicia running down the aisle.

   b. Describe what Nat could have done after Alicia denied his request.

   c. Identify how Nat can support the needs of Baldwin's Hardware.

5. Is Alicia the best person for Nat to talk to about changing his lunch hour? Why?

6. What are the advantages and disadvantages for Nat if he talks with Danielle about changing his lunch hour?

7. What could Alicia do to find her job more appealing?

8. How would you use your self-advocacy skills to construct a presentation that Nat could make to Alicia and separately to Danielle? Write out a dialogue to demonstrate Nat's presentation and how you expect Alicia and Danielle would respond (remember to focus on Alicia's, Danielle's, and Baldwin's needs).

Case #6

Organizational Structure

At every organization there is a chain of command. When you advocate for yourself, it's critical to know who is in charge of specific functions of the organization. Otherwise, you might spend your time trying to persuade the wrong person to help you.

Hipazz Asks, "Who's in Charge?"

Latoya is the manager of "Hipazz," a new music group. She is also the band's bass player. Hipazz signed a contract with Renraw Records to produce two CDs. One CD, "Too Late to Go Home," was completed three months ago. *Billboard, Spin,* and *All About Jazz* magazines gave "Too Late to Go Home" good reviews. *Hip Hop Magazine* said that Hipazz "...may be the next wave for jazz!"

Before becoming a successful musician, Latoya was in foster care in Detroit. While in foster care, she was selected to serve on a youth advisory board for Michigan's Family Independence Agency. She successfully learned about how foster care is organized in Detroit and who the key people were to influence in order to make the system better.

Steve Smoothée is an associate producer for Renraw Records. He promised Latoya that their CD would be well publicized and that promotional tours for the band would be arranged.

In spite of Smoothée's promise, Renraw has done almost no publicity or advertising for "Too Late to Go Home." In addition, they have not arranged any promotional tours or interviews for the group. Latoya is furious. Hipazz has a three-year exclusive contract with Renraw. This means they cannot go to another record company for the remaining time on their contract.

Steve Smoothée is always promising Latoya that he will "work on it," meaning that he will get them more publicity and promotional tours. Nothing happens.

Latoya called her lawyer. Her lawyer told her that the contract is unspecific about publicity. Latoya claimed it was discussed when they signed the contract. Latoya's lawyer said she can sue, but it would be expensive and there is no guarantee they would win.

(continued)

(continued)

Latoya knows that the reviews in *Billboard, Hip-Hop, All About Jazz*, and *Spin* suggest that their album will make money for the company and promote a great interest in their next recording. Latoya believes that if other young groups learn of Renraw's actions, they won't sign with them and Renraw will lose out on finding good new talent.

Latoya realizes that Hipazz and Renraw's goals are complementary (matching). Hipazz needs promotion of their group, a proven moneymaker for Renraw, and Renraw needs to make money and attract more potentially successful groups to their label. Lately, Latoya has come to realize that Steve Smoothée has no influence and she would be wasting her time trying to get him to help.

Questions

1. What are the important facts that relate to the primary challenge of the case?

   a. List Hipazz's **long- and short-term goals.**

   b. Identify Renraw's **needs.**

   c. Identify Smoothée's **needs.**

   d. Describe Latoya's **strengths.**

   e. Identify Hipazz's **allies or supporters.**

   f. Identify **missing information** that would be helpful in planning strategies.

2. What is the **primary challenge** to reaching Hipazz's long-term goal?

3. What **general plan** would you use to get Renraw to promote Hipazz's CD?

4. What reasons might Smoothée have for not promoting Hipazz?

5. If Smoothée will not help Hipazz, why would anyone else at Renraw help Hipazz?

6. How can Latoya find out who at Renraw has the authority and desire to help her group?

7. What reasons might Renraw have to publicize and advertise Hipazz's album?

8. In order to self-advocate to the right person, Latoya must understand how Renraw works. Can you think of all the different departments that are needed to run an organization like Renraw? Think of the functions that are needed, such as sales, promotion, and advertising. What others can you think of?

Accountability

Accountability usually means that a person is identified as responsible for some activity or the results of some activity within an organization.

It doesn't make sense to go to a store and try to return a pair of shoes to the security guard. Therefore, when you advocate for yourself, it is important to understand who on the other side is accountable.

Organizations have many activities and responsibilities. Because these activities are important and because they require other people, machines, and services, one person will be put in charge to manage these activities. That person makes decisions, spends money, makes sure everything goes the way it should, and that everyone involved is doing the right thing. That person is considered "accountable" for the success of that activity, **even if they do not personally do all the activities themselves.**

Taking on accountability often results in special recognition and promotions within the organization. At the same time, if things do not work out, the person in charge will be held "accountable" for problems and failures. This can result in being denied promotions, not receiving a raise in salary, or even being dismissed from a job.

Examples of Accountability

If a school continues to have students perform poorly on academic tests, the principal, Mr. Graham, may be replaced with another person. Even though the principal doesn't teach the classes and isn't directly responsible for the behavior of the students, he will be held accountable for the poor results. In such a situation, the principal may be asked to provide a reason why the results are so poor and a good plan for improving conditions. Mr. Graham may even be given a time limit as to when the results must improve or else he will be replaced.

Accountability occurs even in family life. If Karaar has an eight-year-old child, he is accountable for the health and education of his child. Karaar might want to quit his job until he finds one he really loves, but the loss of income may prevent his child from eating well, having the necessary clothes, or doing well in school. Karaar might want to come home late every night and not help his child with his schoolwork, yet the teacher has told him that his child needs Karaar's help with homework each night. In this case, the accountability is more self-imposed, but nevertheless, Karaar is accountable for his child.

Accountability gets very complicated sometimes. If Karaar's child is in Mr. Graham's school, and Karaar is not helping his child with homework even though the teacher recommended it, is Mr. Graham or Karaar responsible for the child's poor achievement?

Omar Takes on Responsibility and Accountability

When Omar was growing up, his parents told him he would never amount to anything. In so many ways they told Omar, "You can't do anything right." When Omar was a teenager, his parents split up. Neither parent wanted him around. Omar went to a private high school and failed all his subjects except science. He was also caught damaging all the school computers by putting viruses in their systems. His parents were furious and sent him to a boarding school. Omar hated the boarding school and all the other rich kids. In his senior year, his parents gave him a new SUV. He crashed the SUV. His mother and father told him, "Not only can't you do anything right, you are totally irresponsible." They gave him $15,000 and told him never to come home or contact them. Omar decided that life would be better away from his parents.

Omar decided to use the $15,000 to go to college. Throughout Omar's life, he never had to pay for anything and had no idea how to budget his money or even what things cost. He barely made it through the first year because he couldn't afford his own expenses. During his first year at college, Omar decided that the most important thing for him was to have a family and be a parent who would encourage his own children and help them have a happy life.

During his second year at college, Omar decided that he needed to be successfully independent because he had no one else to turn to. He decided to leave college for a time in order to earn enough money to live.

(continued)

(continued)

Omar is determined to return to college, but in the meantime, he wants to make the most of his work. When he left college, he got a job at a supermarket. His only friend from the boarding school teases him about working in a supermarket, "You can't do anything right." Omar is determined to take responsibility for his own life and stop having people tell him he "can't do anything right."

Omar discovered that his manager at the supermarket made a good salary and still had opportunities for promotion. Omar was struck by the fact that the manager had started out as a part-time clerk and advanced in salary and position quickly.

Omar has now worked at an OrgPro supermarket, located in St. Paul, Minnesota, for more than three years in many different jobs. At first he was a stock clerk. His job was to stock shelves with food products and make sure that there were always enough products for customers.

After six months, Omar was promoted to be manager of staples (dry goods or non-perishable items) such as soft drinks, canned goods, cookies, etc. He would place orders when stock (items to be purchased by customers) was low in any of these items. He needed to plan when to order more stock to keep enough products on hand without having too costly an inventory (too much stock that won't be sold for a long time). If inventory went too high, it would cost the store more money. If inventory was too low, it might cost the store in customers, who would go elsewhere to find what they needed.

He did so well as manager of staples that he was promoted to produce manager (vegetables and fruit). His inventory experience was helpful since produce lasts for a very short time. Over-ordering results in spoilage and wasted money and ordering too little results in dissatisfied customers. He also was responsible for purchasing the produce and thus had to select farmers and distributors who would grow good fruits or vegetables, deliver on time, and provide a fair price.

During this entire period, Omar would sometimes fill in at the check-out either as a cashier or bagging the groceries when there was a rush of customers. Through this experience, he became aware of the likes and dislikes of the customers. In just three years, Omar gained comprehensive (wide-ranging) knowledge of how a supermarket works and the skills to make it operate efficiently.

The manager of the store was transferred to a larger store and OrgPro has selected Omar to manage this store. Now Omar will be directly responsible (accountable) for many things. What are they?

Questions

1. After Omar takes the job as store manager, who will be responsible for the following things? Explain who AND why for each situation.

    a. Supervision of the store employees.

    b. Broken arm suffered by Jill, a customer, because Jordan, the shift maintenance person, didn't clean up a jar of mayonnaise dropped by Spencer, another customer.

    c. People getting sick from prepared food purchased from the store.

    d. $500 worth of fruit spoiling because Jasmen, a produce clerk, left it outside in the sun.

    e. Jacklyn, a customer who got food poisoning from canned food.

    f. A shortage of $376 in Josh's cash register at the end of his shift.

    g. Bad weather that keeps customers away from the store.

    h. Paying employees on time.

2. In those situations where Omar is responsible, how will he be held accountable? If, over a three-month period, there are eight reported illnesses from people eating prepared food at Omar's store, what will be the consequences for Omar? Is this fair?

3. Why does someone want to be accountable for responsibilities, such as those Omar has taken on as manager of the supermarket?

4. Katrina wants a job working in produce. Should she speak to Omar or Ms. Laker, the produce manager? Why?

5. Jamad has been working in produce for four years and would like to get a promotion. He realizes there is not much opportunity in produce and is willing to work in other departments. Should he present a request for promotion to Omar or Ms. Laker, the produce manager? Why?

6. Do you think that Omar's experience as a stock clerk, manager of staples, and produce manager are useful for Omar's new job as store manager? Why?

Case #8

Analyzing the Needs of an Organization

Sometimes it seems that your boss will never understand that you deserve more—a salary increase, a vacation, a change in schedule, etc. Analyzing the goals of the organization you work for and demonstrating how your goals will support the organization's goals will help you be a successful self-advocate.

Teresa: Baking for Profit and Pleasure

Teresa works for Phil, a baker in Newark, New Jersey. Her job is to clean the ovens and the store. Sometimes Teresa runs the cash register. Teresa has been working for Phil for four months. She gets paid $6.05 an hour. Teresa does not receive benefits such as vacation or medical coverage.

Phil's bakery specializes in baking eight different types of breads and specialty muffins. His customers mostly work in the neighborhood. When they come in, they enjoy talking with Teresa and often ask her advice on which muffin they should buy. Teresa is Phil's only employee. One of the customers, Jessica, once teased Phil, "You're too old to do all this work—why don't you let this young woman take over?" Phil just scowled and nothing more was said.

When Teresa was twelve, her father became very ill while her mother was in the army. Until she was on her own at 18, Teresa was forced to move many times because her mother was redeployed to different locations. Teresa had to get used to a number of different cities and small towns, different schools, and new friends. In spite of all this moving, Teresa was always able to make one or two friends in each new school.

Overall, Teresa has several long-term personal and career goals. Her primary goal is to be in a position to have a family and provide for her children so that they can have a good education, live in a nice neighborhood, and grow up to be influential members of the community.

Her career goals are to have a steady job that she likes and that will provide some financial security. Teresa likes the baking business but would be open to other types of food retail businesses (retail businesses sell products to individuals).

Teresa has a friend named Jessie who desperately needs a job or she will lose her apartment. Jessie has never worked in a store. Jessie has had some bad breaks. She grew up in a foster home that had five other children. Being the oldest, she had to do all of the housework.

Jessie's foster mother didn't spend much on food so Jessie had to cook a lot of food from very simple ingredients. Jessie became known for her birthday cakes, and a number of local catering companies (companies that sell and deliver food that is already cooked) would buy cakes from her. Not only does Jessie need to keep her apartment but she also wants to start college.

Questions

1. What are the important facts that relate to the primary challenge of the case?

   a. List Teresa's **long- and short-term goals.**

   b. Identify Phil's personal and business **needs.**

   c. Describe Teresa and Jessie's **strengths.**

   d. Identify **missing information** that would be helpful in planning strategies.

2. In one sentence, how would you describe the bakery's mission (strategy or idea of how to make money selling baked foods)?

3. What are three ways that Phil could reach the bakery's mission?

4. The following are four different goals Teresa might have. How could each of Teresa's goals turn into helping Phil meet the bakery's goals? In each case, explain what Teresa must offer to do at the bakery in order to get Phil's support for her goals.

   Specifically:

   a. Teresa wants to get benefits so she can take a one-week vacation without losing her pay.

b. Teresa wants to take a one-year course in bookkeeping at Kennedy Community College. She wants to complete a college degree and become a manager of a food retail business. The course will cost $718. She doesn't have the money. Her friend Edward said that his boss paid for him to take classes in marketing. Edward thinks Teresa should ask Phil to pay for her course.

c. Teresa likes running the cash register. She enjoys working with customers and doesn't like cleaning the ovens. Teresa wants Phil to hire someone else to clean the ovens and let her run the cash register all the time.

d. Teresa wants to help Jessie get a job at Phil's bakery. In the past week, Phil has turned down three other people who asked for jobs, including his cousin's son.

CHAPTER 3

Importance of Your Strengths

Background

It is easier to help someone who is likely to be successful than to help someone who presents him or herself as a problem or a victim. Most people don't want more problems in their lives.

Too often people present problems in order to get attention, such as, "I do not have enough money," or "I have a difficult family." Most people in a position to help you are not persuaded by learning about your problems. If you want support, you need to demonstrate that you have **strengths** that will benefit from support.

When you advocate for yourself, you *must* present your strengths to the other person. This usually requires that you present your accomplishments, your skills, your values, and your future goals. This helps the other person believe that supporting you will result in success. If you stress the **problems,** the other person may think you just attract problems and no matter what support they give you, it will be wasted.

As a successful self-advocate, you must have a good understanding of your own strengths and be able to communicate them to others. You **cannot assume** that others will know or appreciate your strengths. It is your responsibility to inform others of your strengths.

Example

Carla wants to work in the field of hotel management. In one of Carla's informational interviews, she was offered the names of people who might get her an internship at a hotel. The interviewer gave her these names because he was so impressed with Carla's presentation—especially her strengths and the likelihood that she would be a great success.

In her presentations to professionals in the hospitality field (hotels/restaurants), Carla emphasized the fact that she could get along with a variety of different people. She also informed the interviewer that she had taken advantage of a rigorous seminar where she learned self-advocacy, had success at a sales job at an electronics store last summer, and had a passion for working in the hospitality field. Carla also explained how she had dealt with many difficulties in her life and knew what it was like to struggle. Experiencing hardships made Carla determined that nothing would stop her from reaching her goals.

By communicating her strengths, Carla created an impression that if anyone gave her an opportunity, she would turn it into a success.

Concepts to Consider When Presenting Your Strengths

- From time to time, you must do an inventory (specific list) of your strengths. Your strengths may come from experiences you have had, accomplishments you have achieved, personal goals you have established, and recognition you have received from others.

- The process is difficult because it is personal, yet you need to be objective. You cannot be too modest nor can you exaggerate your strengths. To get others to appreciate and understand your strengths, you must be specific.

- Never assume that the other person knows or remembers your accomplishments. You need to let them know about your accomplishments.

Examples of Strengths

- Having clear **long-term goals** is itself a personal strength. Having clear goals demonstrates to others that you are thoughtful, plan ahead, and intend to be successful.

- Your **values** (ideals you believe in) are also personal strengths. Examples of values are

  - Commitment to education

  - Loyalty to friends and family

  - Commitment to group efforts

  - Commitment to helping others in need

  - Involvement in meaningful work

  - Belief in moral values

  - Belief in specific political ideals, such as equal opportunity, civil rights, environment, labor rights, and market economy

  - Keeping promises to others

- **Overcoming obstacles** in your life may be presented as strengths if you have gained some new skills in this struggle. For example, if Josie has lived with two different stepfathers, endured her mother's loss of jobs, and had to transfer to three different high schools in three years, she has probably gained the ability to deal with stress and change as well as different types of people and styles of living.

- Any **positions of responsibility** you have had, such as a job, taking care of a family member, or independently managing areas of your own life, demonstrate an important strength and your ability to carry through with reaching goals.

- Any **specific accomplishments,** such as doing well in a class, sports, community activity, or after school program.

- A particular **personality strength,** such as enjoying people, having a sense of humor, listening well, remembering what others say, tending to look for positive solutions to challenges, etc.

- A particular **skill or thing you are good at doing**. This can be in sports, art, education, or any activity you can think of. For example, you may be very good at getting around your city, cooking food, or taking care of animals.

- **Solving problems** is an important strength. For example, you may be good at resolving disputes with your friends, saving money, or fixing computer problems.

Case #9

Identifying Your Strengths

*When you want support in reaching a goal, it's very tempting to tell the other side all the problems you're having and all the reasons you deserve help. But while the other side may be sympathetic, they will usually feel they can't do much about your problems. To be an effective self-advocate, you must be able to depersonalize (not take it personally) the response you get and focus on presenting your **strengths** and how you can advance the goals of the organization.*

James Asks Lishone for a Raise

James has been working at Hannibal Bookstore on M Street in Washington, D.C. as a clerk for two years. James also helps set up Friday night book readings and discussion groups, when authors read from their books, sign books purchased by customers, and talk to customers.

Just before James's mother became very ill and he went into foster care, she told him that he should read books whenever he had time. She told him her biggest regret was not reading more. That made a big impression on James. Therefore, James really likes working in a bookstore because he loves books and it reminds him of his mother.

James makes $387 a week. His take-home pay (after taxes are taken out of his paycheck) is $324.73 a week. James has to share an apartment because rent is so high. James's monthly expenses are

Rent	415
Food	340
Telephone and utilities	49
Transportation	90
Household items	61
Medical and dental	55
Clothes	49
Personal and health items	37
Savings	50
Entertainment	85
Miscellaneous	<u>67</u>
Total	**$1,298**

(continued)

(continued)

James wants to start taking college business management classes. Someday he would like to manage a bookstore. He would even consider being a manager of one of the bookstores owned by Hannibal. Short-term, James needs to start taking college classes and needs the money to pay for them. Even at the community colleges, it will cost him $378, including books and other educational expenses, for each course.

On Tuesday, James is having coffee with Lishone Rogers, the day shift manager.

James: "Lishone, I need more money."

Lishone: "Don't we all! It seems like it goes faster than we can make it."

James: "Yeah, but I really need more money to pay all my bills."

Lishone: "Yeah, I'm going to so many clubs I can't pay my credit card."

James: "Well, should I talk to anyone about..."

Lishone: "Yeah, talk to Chase Bank. Maybe they'll give you some money. Let's get back to work."

Lishone walks away and James thinks to himself: "Damn this Hannibal Bookstore! They don't care about anyone. Screw them. This is the last time I help them with Friday's book readings."

Questions

1. What are the important facts that relate to the primary challenge of the case?

   a. List James's and Lishone's **long- and short-term goals.**

   b. Identify Lishone's **needs.**

   c. Describe James's **strengths.**

   d. Identify **missing information** that would be helpful in planning strategies.

2. What must James do to get an increase in salary from Hannibal Bookstore?

3. Does Lishone have a real understanding of James's problem? How do you know? What facts support your view?

4. Do you think Lishone understands James's problem from James's perspective, Hannibal Bookstore's perspective, or Lishone's perspective? What facts support your view?

5. Has James done a good job of presenting his strengths? What facts support your view?

6. What are some of James's core values (things he believes in strongly)? Can these be considered strengths? Why?

7. Has James done a good job of identifying and describing his goal? Explain. In your answer, refer specifically to what James communicated and what you think he might have left out.

8. Is James taking Hannibal Bookstore's lack of interest in his problem personally? Does it matter? Explain your answer in detail.

Exercise #3

Presenting Your Strengths

Never assume that the other person knows or remembers your strengths. You need to let others know about your strengths when you advocate for yourself. Write answers to the following questions and keep them for future use. It's a good idea to review and revise (change and/or add new strengths) your answers every three to six months.

1. Identify at least three personal strengths:

   (Look over the chapter introduction and see how many of the following personal strengths you can think of.)

   - What are your personal or professional goals?

   - Explain some strong values you have.

   - Identify some positions of responsibility you have had.

   - Think of some specific accomplishments you have achieved.

   - List things you are good at doing.

   - List some of your personality strengths.

   - Identify some of the obstacles you have had to overcome in your life.

   - Identify some difficult problems you have solved.

2. Do you let others know about strengths?

   - In the past, how have you let others (family, friends) know about these strengths and successes?

   - How have you let people in authority (teachers, social workers, bosses, or others) know about these strengths and successes?

3. What is the best way to let people know about your past success?

   - Think of when you first meet a teacher, a job supervisor, or a person who might want to help you. What is the best way to let people know about your strengths and past successes?

4. What personal strengths do you want to develop?

   - When thinking about long-term goals, most people discover there are personal areas they want to develop. Improving specific skills and developing more knowledge and experiences in particular areas are some ways to improve your strengths. What strengths do you want to develop?

CHAPTER 4

Making Transitions[1]

Background

If you want to be successful and independent, you will make many important *transitions* in your life. There is a difference between making a *change* and making a *transition*. If you make a physical change without going through the process of transition, the goals you had for making the change will most likely never be met.

Throughout your life, you will want to make many changes even if they are difficult to make. If you fail to make a change, it may not be because you "really didn't want to make the change," but rather that you didn't understand the process of transitions.

A transition takes more time than a change, but it usually has more meaning and lasts longer than just a physical change.

Example

At a high school graduation, someone will usually give a speech about how on this day students are now adults with adult responsibilities and opportunities. However, the transition to becoming an independent adult takes much more time: time to separate from the high school life style, time to think about and experiment with making future goals, and time to start new endeavors (activities) in your life. While most people want the change from high school student to adult to happen completely on graduation day, it doesn't come about all at once. To be successful, you must understand the process of transition and devote time to making endings, experimenting with new ideas, and beginning new activities.

(continued)

---

[1] This chapter has been inspired by the work of William Bridges, Ph.D., author of *Transitions: Making Sense of Life's Changes,* and was developed with support from the Andrus Family Fund.

(continued)

Look at these examples and identify the attempted change and try to explain **why** the change did not last:

- Bernice is 22 years old. From 12:00 p.m. to 8:00 p.m. six days a week, Bernice works as an airport baggage handler. She likes work, loves sleeping late, and enjoys going out with her friends. Since she was 15, Bernice wanted to have a family and make enough money to support her children. To reach her goals, Bernice **decides she needs a college education.** She begins college by taking one morning course, three times a week before work. After midterms, the professor informs her that if she does not do more research, she will fail the class. The library is open for research until 11:00 p.m. every evening, but Bernice has many friends she enjoys hanging out with after work from 8:00 p.m. to 11:00 p.m.

- **Malcolm decides he will take better care of his health and will exercise for 90 minutes every day.** He is successful for two weeks but then becomes terribly bored and tired. He tried to include his exercise routine without eliminating anything else he was doing. He probably will not make it through the third week without giving up his exercise.

- **Tiebauld** is 19 years old. He has lived in foster care for six years. His social worker points out that his anger gets him in trouble. At his group home, he is put on notice that if he doesn't change his behavior, he will be put on restriction. For the next six weeks, **Tiebauld is real "nice." He makes sure he never challenges any of the staff in the group home.** One day a staff member unfairly accuses Tiebauld of purposely missing his counseling session. Actually, Tiebauld was held after school by his English teacher, who offered to help him enter a writing contest. Tiebauld explodes, throws everything off the staff member's desk, and curses him out.

In each of these cases, the person makes a change and then cannot seem to stick with it. What prevented each person from sticking with his or her change?

What Are "Transitions"?

You will want to make changes throughout your life. Even though you want to or need to make changes that are good for you, these changes are often difficult or impossible to accomplish without going through a process (a number of small steps).

A change in action alone is not enough for the change to last or be beneficial. Therefore, you need to learn a process that will make the change last and be useful for your goals. This process is called a **transition.** The ability to make a good change that lasts requires that you change your thinking as well as your actions and that you become aware of the entire process.

Most Difficult Part of Transitions

Bernice, Malcolm, and Tiebauld made changes in their actions but not in their thinking. All three were looking forward to change, but they failed to make a transition that would make their changes last. They failed because *they did not give up something in their present lives.* None of them recognized that they would have to give up something in their present lives to make a successful transition. Maybe they made the mistake of assuming that they could change, and at the same time, stay the same. Perhaps they didn't realize that they had to let go of something in order to make the transitions they desired.

Failure to Give Up Something in Their Present Lives

- Bernice's social life was very important to her. The recognition (respect, affection, friendliness) of her friends made her feel good. If she gave that up, she might have to take time to find different friends that supported her college goals. Perhaps she was afraid that no one else would recognize that she was smart and fun to be with.

- Malcolm was not willing to think differently about his present life and desire for exercise. He was not yet willing to give up 90 minutes of present activity for something he really wanted.

- Tiebauld understood that his anger was trouble and probably knew he had to start thinking differently as well as being "nice." He was further along in the endings zone than the other two people, but he did not think about why it was so hard to give up his anger. Perhaps his anger made him feel less controlled by others and giving it up would make him feel weak or vulnerable. There was something he needed from his anger, and until he figured this out and found a replacement, he would not be able to control his anger for very long.

The Three Zones of Transition

The three zones of transition are

- Endings Zone

- Neutral Zone

- New Beginnings Zone

When you make a transition, something inside of you changes. This takes time. This time can be divided into three stages or *zones*. You may be in each zone at different times or at the same time. For example, it is natural to be in the endings zone and starting the neutral zone at the same time.

First Zone: Endings Zone

The **endings zone** is the biggest challenge!

As you go through life, you cannot move ahead without ending or leaving something behind. This ending often creates fear. Are you making a BIG mistake?

The process of ending is painful and difficult. Your identity (who you are) is tied to your present and your past. If you end something, you will lose some of your identity—how you think of yourself. This will make you feel uncertain about yourself. Endings are scary. Therefore, you may not want to deal with them. Endings may also make you feel that you are admitting that you made a mistake because you are moving on from something you had needed or wanted in the past.

To move ahead with a transition, the goal is to let go of the person you used to be and find the new person you will become in a new situation. To move ahead, you have to adjust your identity. For example, Bernice must begin to think of herself as a college student and give up the identity she gets from just hanging out.

Too often people fool themselves by thinking that endings are easy, or that they have made an ending when they have not. Look at how hard it was for Bernice, Malcolm, and Tiebauld.

These are some things people have done to help themselves get through the endings zone:

- Identify **what you will lose** by making this ending.

- Understand the **reason** you need to make the ending.

- Identify **changes** you will have to make in your behavior and attitudes.

- Mark the endings (do something special to **celebrate** or honor the ending).

- Treat your past with **respect** (you may want the ending, but you must not put down where you have been in your past).

Second Zone: Neutral Zone

Making an ending frees you to come up with some good ideas for the new beginnings you want. By making the ending, you can now think freely and creatively about the new beginnings you want to take. Be patient; new beginnings will *not* just magically appear but will take time to develop.

This period between making an ending and starting a new beginning is called the **neutral zone**. You may stay in this zone longer than the endings or new beginnings zones. This is a wonderful period for relying on your own creative energy. During the time you are in the neutral zone, you may feel confused or that your life is upside down. Maybe you cannot see any purpose. But this is natural, and this confusion helps you come up with important and lasting new directions for your life.

Possibly the hardest part of being in the neutral zone is being patient. You must be patient when you feel confusion or chaos because your creativity comes during times when you are most uncertain and confused. If you want to find solutions and answers to important questions in your life, you need to encourage your creativity and explore all paths to new beginnings. Do not be afraid to be confused. There will be many new and complex thoughts in your head, and you just need to be patient and believe that in the future it will all make sense. Do not expect to understand everything that goes on during the neutral zone.

These are some things people have done to help themselves get through the neutral zone:

- Make a journal of your experiences and how you feel about them.

- Find specific times and good places for being alone. Advice from friends and authority figures are fine, but in the end, you need to analyze and use what advice makes sense to you.

- Think of how your understanding of your life has changed throughout your life. For example, look at something you once did and thought was so important, but now is not so important. This doesn't mean that what you once did wasn't important, just that your understanding of it has changed. This shows that you have the ability to change your thinking.

Third Zone: New Beginnings

New beginnings are scary. You become a new person. As you enter a new beginning, you have new understandings, new values, new attitudes, and, most of all, new identities.

These are some things people have done to help themselves get through the new beginning zone:

- Explain the basic reason you are making this transition.
- Paint a picture of how the outcome will look and feel.
- Make a step-by-step plan for phasing in the outcome of the transition.

MAKING TRANSITIONS

ENDINGS ZONE

Importance

- Without endings, you cannot
  - Move ahead with your life
  - Make a permanent or beneficial change
  - Become a new person

Feelings

- Pain
- Difficulty
- Uncertainty about your identity
- Resistance to endings
- Fearfulness of loss of identity
- Denial of importance of ending(s)
- Fear of having made a mistake
- Loss of something familiar
- Disengagement, disidentification, disenchantment, disorientation

Useful Tools for Getting Through This Zone

- Identify what you will lose by making the ending
- Understand reasons for making the ending
- Identify changes you will have to make in behavior and attitude
- Celebrate or honor the ending
- Treat your past with respect; do not put it down

NEUTRAL ZONE

Importance

- Prepare for new beginnings
- Encourage great creativity
- Explore all paths to new beginnings

Feelings

- Extreme confusion
- Life is upside down
- Life has lost its purpose
- Enjoyment of creative process

Useful Tools for Getting Through This Zone

- Make a journal of experiences and how you feel about them
- Spend time alone
- Write autobiography and discover how your perceptions of the past have changed
- Find out what you really want
- Identify what would be unlived in your life if you went to Mars tomorrow

NEW BEGINNINGS ZONE

Importance

- Become the person you want to be
- Take more control of your life

Feelings

- Scared
- Feel like a new person
- Gaining:
  - New understandings
  - New values
  - New attitudes
  - New identities

Useful Tools for Getting Through This Zone

- Paint a picture of how the outcome will look and feel
- Explain the purpose of what you are looking for
- Make a step-by-step plan for phasing in the outcome

Case #10

Transitions

Everyone experiences the transitions process when they make successful and lasting changes. While going through the transitions process is similar, each person does it in a different way. To understand the process, the "Making Transitions" chart is separated into three zones (stages); however, most people experience being in more than one zone at any one time. In this next case, see if you can find evidence to demonstrate the different zones each character is in and what they do to move through the zone. Remember, any character can be in more than one zone at a time.

Fabiola: From Change to Transition

Chapter One: Getting There

At 8:19 a.m., Fabiola found herself on Fifth Avenue and 59th Street in New York City. The neighborhood was unfamiliar. People were hurrying in and out of a white skyscraper over 55 stories high. Fabiola checked an address scribbled on a card. It matched that of the skyscraper, but Fabiola walked away. Why was she here? She had an appointment for an informational interview with a computer security company.

This appointment frightened her. What was the point? She had graduated high school two years ago. She had had three different jobs since then. After graduation she worked at servicing computers at a large advertising company. The job was not interesting. All she did was plug in computers. She was promised a promotion, but when the company had financial troubles, Fabiola was the first to be let go. It took three months to get her next job at a messenger service.

At the messenger service, Fabiola worked as an expediter, arranging for the deliveries of packages. She quit this job because it was boring. She now works as a sales clerk in a clothing store. This job doesn't excite her either. She likes clothes but hates helping rude customers. Three months ago, she moved out of her mother's apartment into her own apartment. The situation at home was really bad and she had to get out.

With only 11 minutes before her scheduled appointment, Fabiola was now more than a block away and walking in the wrong direction. Fabiola was thinking she had made a mistake, a big mistake, in leaving home.

Could it be that it hadn't been so bad when she lived at home? She remembers hating living at home. Now she felt different. This change in her thinking added to her confusion. She didn't have high rent to pay when she lived with her mother. She had lots of friends. Often she was able to save money to go to some clubs and buy great clothes. But now that she was independent, Fabiola was struggling to pay her bills. Independence seemed to require more than just moving out.

If she made her appointment today, this would be her fifth informational interview. She remembered her feelings when she was fired from the advertising company. For months she felt anxious and angry with everyone. She never wanted to feel that way again. Even though her present job was nothing great, she was hesitant to try anything different. Someone had told her that if she wanted to get far in computers, she would either have to go to college or take some advanced computer training. Fabiola did not like the idea of being a student again.

Fabiola watched the people on the street. They seemed important. She watched a truck go by. Its sign read "Computer Services." Fabiola wondered about the kinds of jobs they were heading to. She heard a different voice inside her head. It told her to turn around and go to her informational interview. She had five minutes to be on time.

Fabiola stopped and looked back at the full height of the white skyscraper. Everything seemed confusing. She would like to work with computers, but she also thought her life was a failure and she was too far behind. She thought about all the people streaming into the building. They seemed to have a purpose. What was hers?

Fabiola entered the white skyscraper. The entrance ceiling was three or four stories high. Well-dressed security guards stood behind marble counters. There were lines of people in front of each security person. Everyone was in a hurry to get where they were going. Fabiola waited in a line. When it was her turn, the security guard asked her where she was going. "Janet Robinson, Security Designs." The guard called to confirm Fabiola's appointment. "Take the third elevator to the 44th floor."

The elevator raced to the 44th floor. Fabiola found herself in a large reception area. She was impressed with the three large sofas and a beautiful wooden table with magazines on it. The receptionist was a young man. He wore a suit and tie. He seemed very professional. He asked Fabiola who she was here to see. "Janet Robinson, I have an 8:30 appointment. My name is Fabiola Lewison."

"Have a seat Ms. Lewison. I'll tell Ms. Robinson you're here. Would you like some coffee or water?"

(continued)

(continued)

Fabiola sat on a beautiful white sofa. She had little experience with anyone calling her "Ms. Lewison" with respect. Fabiola thought the receptionist had confused her with someone else. She was so confused she didn't reply to the receptionist's offer. The same thought came back to her, "What's the use? When the receptionist leaves his desk, I'll get out of here fast."

Chapter Two: Thinking About the Past

Maybe her present job as a sales clerk in the clothing store was not so bad. Fabiola knew everyone who worked at the store and she had a number of friends. Other clerks thought she was funny. If she stayed another four months, she would get a raise. Maybe she could afford her studio apartment if she offered to share it with a friend. The work wasn't all that hard and she liked the hours—1:00 p.m. to 8:30 p.m. She didn't have to wake up early. What was the point of trying something harder and more demanding? She would probably fail, and then she would really be mad at herself.

Waiting for Ms. Robinson gave Fabiola time to think about her life. She was confused because her past always seemed to be a bit different whenever she thought about it. In the past, things had always seemed rough for Fabiola. Her family had very little money and needed help from relatives and sometimes the government. Her mother suffered depression when her first marriage broke up and used drugs for a number of years. During that time, Fabiola was placed in foster care. She was 16. Fabiola remained in foster care until she was 19. She was placed in two different group homes and transferred to three different high schools.

Fabiola was fortunate to be able to leave the foster care system at 19 and return to her home. Yet, she remembers being scared about leaving foster care. But when she returned home, it was different. Her mother no longer used drugs and was not as depressed. Her mother had married another man with whom she had two children.

Even though Fabiola had moved home, she rarely saw her mother or stepfather. Her mother worked late into the night and her stepfather had two jobs. They seemed to care about Fabiola but never had time for her. When Fabiola moved home, she had to look after her younger stepbrother and stepsister. This took a lot of time. Sometimes she even thought foster care was easier. All this made Fabiola more confused.

Fabiola picked up a magazine about computers. The receptionist was answering phone calls. Fabiola thought of herself as smart, but now things seemed to make no sense. She continued to think about her past. Fabiola's stepfather and mother had little time to help Fabiola understand her own strengths. In foster care no one told her she was good at anything. They always seemed more concerned with her problems. At school Fabiola never got good grades, although a few teachers told her she was smart and had "promise." But no one ever told her what to do with "promise."

Fabiola's experiences with being on her own had given her great strengths, but Fabiola really had no idea how she could use them to become successful and reach some of her dreams. She had taken a self-advocacy seminar and learned how to use informational interviews to gain knowledge about the opportunities that were out there. She had already done four of these interviews. The last interviewer helped her set up this meeting.

She had had a tough home life, but she was beginning to think it was a mistake to leave it so soon. Her younger stepbrother and stepsister were family and loved her, and even her stepfather could be fun. Maybe it hadn't been all that bad.

Thoughts whirled through her head: too many jobs, too many ideas about what she should do with her life, and too many regrets about leaving her family and other jobs. Maybe she should go back home, help her mother with the younger children, and wait until she was more ready to be on her own. Maybe this informational interview would help her find the answer.

Chapter Three: A Transitions Story

Fabiola stared at the receptionist. There was a pause in phone calls and he noticed her stare. He said, "None of my friends or family believe it. At this time two years ago, I was nowhere. Nothing mattered then."

The receptionist walked to a window and pointed outside. "Trouble was all around me then. I was in high school. Everyone was on my case. Teachers, guidance counselors, social workers, and especially the assistant principal. Fought them all. No one was going to push me around. Spent so much time fighting, I never did schoolwork or thought of my future."

Fabiola didn't know what to say, and for a long time the receptionist just looked out the window in silence. He continued, "I didn't do anything for a year after I graduated. Finally, I realized I missed high school! Strange. Just couldn't get going until I realized that high school life was over."

The receptionist walked back to his desk. "Now I have a job. I'll be a fraud investigator in four years. I have a job that pays the bills."

Chapter Four: The Informational Interview

The receptionist answered a call. After hanging up the phone, he asked Fabiola to come with him. Fabiola did not know why, but she followed the receptionist rather than catch the next elevator to freedom.

(continued)

(continued)

They went down a hallway into a large room with many cubicles. Each cubicle had computers. Some cubicles were empty, others had a number of people looking at the screens, and many had just one person working on a computer.

The receptionist led Fabiola to one of the cubicles. A woman wearing a blue suit and white blouse was standing in front of the cubicle and explaining something to a group of people. When the woman wearing the white blouse saw Fabiola, she told the group they would have to meet later. She suggested to Fabiola that they go to the conference room. Fabiola felt a wave of excitement at seeing all these professionals working with computers.

Fabiola was stunned by the time they reached the conference room. Everything was happening fast. Would she be able to say anything? She remembered advice from the self-advocacy seminar and took out her agenda.

"I'm a bit nervous, excuse me." Fabiola decided to just begin at the beginning of her agenda. "I am very pleased that you have time for me. My goal is to have a career in computer security. Mr. Hightower told me that you started Security Designs. He told me that you are very experienced in computer security. I want to work in the field of information security. Your advice would be extremely useful."

Ms. Robinson asked Fabiola to talk a little about her interests and her background. Fabiola explained her interests in computer security and tried to communicate her strengths. Ms. Robinson was very serious. Fabiola wasn't sure if Ms. Robinson was interested in her.

Ms. Robinson asked Fabiola why she had so many jobs lately. Unfortunately, Fabiola had not planned a response to this obvious question. "Well... guess I was having a hard time finding myself." This honest response encouraged Ms. Robinson to talk about her own life.

Chapter Five: The Informational Interview Continues— Another Transitions Story

For eight years, Ms. Robinson had worked for an accounting firm. She became their best computer expert. Everyone treated her with respect. Her boss gave her bonuses and sent her on exciting trips. Yet, Ms. Robinson felt her work had no purpose. She did not like working alone. She started to think about opening her own company, but she was afraid. She feared giving up everyone's respect and her high salary. She was good at her work but was afraid she would not have the skills to manage her own company.

Ms. Robinson had realized that her life as a computer expert was good, but it was not what she wanted. She had to end this chapter. Yet after she quit her job, she thought she had made a horrible mistake. She got a few temporary jobs to support herself. She was worried and dazed. She talked with many people in the computer, accounting, and finance fields. She got different ideas for starting a business, but none of them seemed right. She thought about giving up computer work and becoming an actress.

A young woman politely interrupted them and asked Ms. Robinson if she could submit a quotation to a client for a year of security work. Ms. Robinson looked at the quotation. She noted that intrusion detection had been left out. Fabiola didn't understand all these new terms, but she was enjoying herself. Ms. Robinson's story had an effect on her. She did not feel as alone.

Ms. Robinson picked up her story. For four months, she was so confused that she hardly worked or left home. She continued to feel she had made a horrible mistake. During the end of that four-month period, Ms. Robinson began to realize how much she wanted to investigate security breaches. She joined the Computer Security Institute and read everything about computer security. She learned that this type of work would allow her to meet more people. Finally, she used the advice she had been given and all that she had read to develop a plan for how she could reach her goals.

"I know you didn't want to hear my life story. But I want you to know that we all struggle to reach our dreams. My advice: Start thinking of yourself as an information specialist. Once you start seeing yourself differently, things will be easier. What you have done is great, but now you are ready to move on."

The meeting stretched to an hour. Fabiola met some computer specialists and saw the work they did. Her sense of confusion was losing out to excitement. At the end of the meeting, Ms. Robinson suggested that with the information Fabiola was gathering she should begin to develop a plan. She also urged her to accept what she had already done in her life but move on to a new beginning. Ms. Robinson hinted that she might be willing to help Fabiola find a job or internship when she was ready.

Questions

Read the story carefully. Think about the differences and similarities of how each character handles the transition zones. Read the following questions. Then read the story again and underline any evidence that supports a character being in any of the three zones. Use the "Making Transitions" chart to help you identify evidence. In the margin next to your underlined evidence, indicate to which stage the evidence applies.

You have been assigned to one of two groups: *Group One* or *Group Two*.

Group One

Answer the following questions:

1. In the case there is evidence that Fabiola, the receptionist, and Ms. Robinson each have experiences being in the **endings zone.**

   a. What evidence is there that Fabiola and the receptionist are in the endings zone?

   b. How did Ms. Robinson get out of the ending zone?

2. What specific advice would you give Fabiola to help her be more successful while in the **neutral zone?**

3. Fabiola has decided to become a computer security professional. She has enrolled in college part-time and got an entry-level job at Security Designs. How would you advise Fabiola to effectively deal with this **new beginnings zone?**

Group Two

Answer the following questions:

1. Fabiola, the receptionist, and Ms. Robinson have experience in the **neutral zone.**

   a. What evidence is there that Fabiola and the receptionist are in the neutral zone?

   b. How did Ms. Robinson get out of the neutral zone?

2. What specific advice would you give Fabiola to help her be more successful while in the **endings zone?**

3. Fabiola has decided to become a computer security professional. She has enrolled in college part-time and got an entry-level job at Security Designs. How would you advise Fabiola to effectively deal with this **neutral zone?**

Finding Mentors and Allies

Background

Mentors

Throughout life, you need to learn new things. One of the ways to learn is through someone who has greater experience and knowledge than you have in certain areas. These people can help you a great deal by teaching you (mentoring) what you need to know to help you achieve your goals and save time. These people who share their experiences and knowledge with you are called **mentors**.

Example of a Mentor

In her first year at college, Ahote got an internship at a law firm, Williams, Thomas & Clinton. She helped paralegals review contracts. Her job was to make sure the contracts were complete and no pages were missing. While her job was not difficult, the supervisor of the department noticed that she did it well, was extremely responsible, and would not leave work until she completed each day's assignment.

As Ahote got to know her supervisor, Mr. Dillard, she discovered that he began working at the age of 16 and was unable to go to college until he was 27 because his family was so poor. He knew what it was like to struggle when first starting out. Ahote began to ask Mr. Dillard for career advice. They developed a bond, and he offered to help her any way he could. Mr. Dillard devoted a good deal of time explaining how to handle college work and what classes Ahote should take to prepare for a career in law. In return, Ahote did her job well and made sure that Mr. Dillard recognized how valuable and appreciated his advice was to her about planning and college work.

(continued)

(continued)

Near the end of her internship, Ahote learned of an honors pre-law class at her college for second-year students. In order to get into the class, she had to have a recommendation from someone who knew her in a work situation. Ahote asked Mr. Dillard for a recommendation, which he gladly wrote. His recommendation was very complimentary, and his title of "Director of Paralegals" made a big impression on the selection committee for the honors class. Ahote was accepted.

Mr. Dillard is a good example of a mentor and an ally.

Allies

In self-advocacy, you want to persuade people in authority to change their positions and give you assistance. In addition to your self-advocacy presentation, your effectiveness, and communicating your strengths, you will also benefit if you can demonstrate that others support your position. These people who support your position are called **allies**.

Example of an Ally

Alfredo works as an electrician's assistant for Wyly Electricians, Inc. His job is to connect outlets and switches. He works with three different master electricians. Alfredo has the best relationship with Linda, one of the master electricians, who has worked for the company for 11 years. Linda has been very helpful in teaching Alfredo how to make secure and safe connections. On breaks, they often talk about music and sports and enjoy each other's company. When the boss has extra overtime jobs, Linda always requests that Alfredo be given first choice.

On a recent job, the customer accused "the electricians," specifically Alfredo, of stealing his watch that he left on the bathroom sink. The manager of Wyly told Alfredo he would be fired unless he returned the watch. This was extremely unfair because Alfredo was assumed guilty without any evidence. When Alfredo explained that he didn't steal the watch, the manager fired him.

Alfredo wanted the manager to reconsider, but he couldn't get him to listen. He told Linda what happened and asked if she could get the manager to listen to his explanation that the customer was mistaken. Linda stopped work and called the manager. She told him that he was a "coward to take the word of the customer over Alfredo's. Alfredo is the best assistant Wyly has ever had and there is no way he would steal anything. If you don't immediately rehire him and apologize, I'll quit."

Linda is an exceptional example of an ally.

Concepts to Consider When Briefing These Cases

When working with the following cases, think about these concepts:

- All successful people have mentors. A mentor is someone who has advanced experiences and a desire to help you. A mentor is similar to a teacher or an advisor who supports your efforts to achieve your goals. Some people think of a mentor as a coach—someone who cares about you and is willing to share knowledge and experience to provide instruction and advice.

- Finding and maintaining a good mentor usually takes considerable effort on your part. You must reach out and create a relationship that will support some of the mentor's needs.

- An ally is someone who believes in you and will support you in your goals.

- Many people enjoy becoming allies for others. Allies can help by

  - Connecting you with others who help you in reaching your goals

  - Serving as references for your skills and abilities

  - Presenting your position to others

  - Adding support to your position in difficult advocacy situations

- Your allies can be teachers, group leaders, friends, relatives, work colleagues (people you work with), past employers, etc.

- You should not be shy about asking your allies for help, but at the same time, you should ask for help that your allies could easily give. For example, if you need a recommendation from an ally, give the person all the information he or she will need to write it. Think of how you can save him or her time and effort so that helping you is as easy as possible.

Case #11

Identifying Potential Mentors and Allies

When you develop a new goal or want to try something different, a mentor or an ally can be extremely useful. This is true at any age and for any occupation. The successful self-advocate identifies people who could be useful mentors and effective allies.

David Moves Ahead

David Jackson works as a master plumber for Smooth Flow Plumbers in St. Louis, Missouri. David is 31 years old and has two daughters in elementary school. His wife works as an accountant for an insurance company. She works part-time in order to be at home for the children when they get out of school.

David grew up in a very tough neighborhood. He had some trouble with the law when he sold stolen merchandise. He had a rocky start after getting his GED. For three years, he couldn't get any better job than working for moving companies. Then he was lucky enough to get into an apprenticeship plumbing program. He worked hard and worked his way up to master plumber. Just two years ago, David graduated college.

David has met many people through his work. Two of the wealthier customers he worked for, Hilary Jones and Stone Caruthers, told him they were so impressed with his work and reliability that they would help him if he ever wanted to start his own company. Hillary and Stone were in such different worlds that David never took them seriously. He knew that Hillary was a successful money manager and that her apartment was worth at least two million dollars. Stone was a very successful real estate developer.

In his work, David has met some very competent carpenters, sheet rockers, painters, and electricians. Over the years, he has learned to spot the best craftspeople in all the different building trades.

When he was at college studying business management, a professor suggested that David think of opening his own contracting business. He could do home renovations and perhaps build new homes if he combined his knowledge of construction and management.

At college, David learned that if you had a good idea and made a good business plan, you could often borrow or raise money to start a business. He knows that his wife's boss began her insurance business with a business plan and a loan from a bank.

David has decided to open his own construction business but needs help in developing a business plan and finding ways to borrow or raise money.

Questions

1. What are the important facts that relate to the primary challenge of the case?

    a. List David's **long- and short-term goals.**

    b. Identify Hilary's and Stone's **needs.**

    c. Describe David's **strengths.**

    d. Identify David's **allies or supporters.**

    e. Identify **missing information** that would be helpful in planning strategies.

2. What is the **primary challenge** that David must face to start his own construction business?

3. How can Hilary and Stone help David?

4. How can David's wife's boss help David?

5. How can David's friends who are craftspeople help David?

6. What is the best way for David to approach each of these people to get their advice and knowledge?

7. What transitional zone is David in, and why do you think he is in that zone? Why is this zone particularly important for David? What can he do to help himself get through this zone? Finally, is there any evidence that David is in, or has passed through, any other transitional zone?

Case #12

Establishing a Mentorship

All successful people have mentors. Most people have different mentors at different times in their lives. Successful people know how to develop mentoring relationships. In some cultures and situations, mentors are assigned to people. Yet many of us need to search out our own mentors.

Jasda Needs a Mentor

Jasda has been working at the AirEx shipping center near the South Portland, Maine airport for the past eight months. His job is to load and unload trucks. It takes him more than an hour by bus to get from his home in North Portland to his job. He rents a small room from his aunt. His aunt and her three small children live in the same apartment, and Jasda finds it quite crowded.

The work at AirEx is hard, the hours are awful, and the pay is okay, but not great for planning an independent future. Jasda is 21 years old. He wants to someday have his own apartment and family. He wants to make sure his children never have to live in foster care as he did for five years. While in foster care, Jasda lived in eight different placements. He had seven different social workers. He had to deal with a lot of different people and challenging situations. Yet, he still managed to graduate from high school and get this job.

Jasda likes shipping as a career. Someday he would like to be a regional manager of a shipping center for a large city or even another country. He knows that it will take management training, a degree in business, and "knowing the right people."

During the past two months, Jasda has met Ms. Greer a couple of times. Ms. Greer is the evening supervisor of plant operations. The rumor is that Ms. Greer came from a very rich family. When Ms. Greer was 17, her mother died and her father lost all his money. Ms. Greer accomplished everything on her own. At 17, she completed high school and also had a part-time job to support her father. Things were tough, so she had to work after high school and went to college at night. It took her seven years to get her college degree in business management.

Ms. Greer is very serious and strict with the workers. Yet she seems fair and always will listen to someone who has a problem. Ms. Greer is 42 years old and has two children. She is being considered for a promotion to Director of Operations for Airfreight. Jasda is very interested in working specifically in the area of airfreight.

Jasda could save a great deal of time if he could get advice from an experienced professional such as Ms. Greer. If he develops a good relationship with Ms. Greer, she could be an important reference for future promotions and help him make contacts with others who could be helpful to Jasda's career.

Questions

1. What are the important facts that relate to the primary challenge of the case?

   a. List Jasda's **long- and short-term goals.**

   b. Identify Ms. Greer's **needs** and the needs of AirEx.

   c. Describe Jasda's **strengths.**

   d. Identify **missing information** that would be helpful in planning strategies.

2. What does Jasda need to do to reach his goal of becoming a manager in the field of shipping?

3. Why would Ms. Greer want to be a mentor for Jasda?

4. What is an approach that Jasda can use to interest Ms. Greer in being his mentor?

5. What would Jasda have to do to continue a mentoring relationship with Ms. Greer?

6. Describe a mentoring experience you have had.

7. What transitional zone is Jasda in, and why do you think he is in that zone? Why is this zone particularly important for Jasda? How can he help himself get through this zone? Finally, is there any evidence that Jasda is in, or has passed through, any other transitional zone?

8. Is Jasda's job a dead end, or does it have potential for a career?

CHAPTER 6

Depersonalizing Issues and Recognizing the Needs of Others

Background

If you allow yourself to get angry, overreact, and lose control, you will never reach your goals.

It is natural to become personally involved when you are trying to reach your goals. If someone is not very helpful or obstructs your progress toward a goal, it is easy to get angry and lose control.

If someone appears hostile or unsupportive, you must not assume that such an attitude is a reaction to you. You need to depersonalize (not take personally) the situation and focus on your goals rather than the other person's attitude.

When you feel like getting angry, remember to rely on your self-advocacy skills and stick to the issues, facts, and rational reasons for your requests and remember to find ways to help the other person accomplish his or her goals.

It can be a challenge to figure out the needs and motivations of the other person. For example, Alvin works as a cashier. He wants more overtime hours, but all his co-workers tell him his boss gets furious when anyone wants more overtime. Alvin has a choice:

1. He can ask for overtime and be angry with his boss for being unsupportive of his needs.

2. He can ask his boss for overtime and not get upset when his boss gets angry.

3. Or, he can understand that the boss's anger about overtime is not personal and try to figure out if there is anything Alvin can offer to do that would make getting overtime something his boss would support.

Option #1 is not a good option because Alvin is taking the boss's anger personally. Option #2 suggests that at least Alvin is not taking the situation personally. However, option #3 is the best option because Alvin is not taking the boss's anger personally and is using his self-advocacy training to try to determine how to support the boss's needs.

Discovering the needs of others is essential in self-advocacy. You cannot get others to support your goals unless you understand their needs and connect their needs with helping you reach your goals. Even when the other person does not appear supportive, if you can figure out the other person's needs and goals, you will have a better chance of reaching your own goals.

Example

In his second year of college, Trevor was doing very well in his honors marketing class. He was also enjoying and doing well in his English and even his biology classes. He liked his psychology class and felt it was very useful for a career in marketing. However, he was struggling in the class. He got a "C" on his midterm exam and needed to get an "A" on his final exam to get a "B" for the class and maintain his overall "B+" average.

Trevor studied for two weekends for his final and got extra help from a senior. He knew the material and was likely to get an "A." When the grades were posted, there was a note that some students had clearly cheated because answers were very similar. Because the teacher did not want to hurt anyone by giving a failing grade, he gave anyone suspected of cheating a final grade of a "C-." Trevor was in this category.

Trevor was furious. He knew he got at least a "B+," if not an "A," on the test. He also knew that he would lose his scholarship if his overall grade average went below a "B+." This was serious for him and could ruin his chance to remain in college. Trevor had not cheated. This was unfair.

Although Trevor wanted to storm into the professor's office, tell him off, and threaten to complain to the Dean, he waited and planned a rational self-advocacy approach. He made an appointment with the professor. He explained his career goals, the importance of college in his life, the fact that he was going to be a successful graduate of the college, and how he had studied for the test, especially after doing poorly on the midterm. Trevor even discussed some of the principles of psychology he had learned in the class. He concluded by agreeing that cheating represented a big problem, and that he could understand that the professor was in a difficult position in tracking it down. He offered to take another exam to demonstrate that he had not cheated.

The professor was impressed with Trevor and took out his exam and reviewed it again. He recognized that Trevor could not have cheated. He changed his test grade to an "A" and gave him a final class grade of "B." While Trevor was still angry about how he had been treated, he achieved his goal of getting his grade changed and removing the stigma of cheating.

Concepts to Consider When Working with These Cases

- In most self-advocacy situations, the other person responds to your request for help on "rational" grounds. That means that you need to help the other person understand a reason why supporting you will help reach his or her objectives.

- In most self-advocacy situations, the other person is more interested in the reason to support your request than whether he or she likes you.

- Rejection of your request is more likely based on reasons other than whether a person likes you. Liking or disliking you plays a role, but it is usually not the main reason someone accepts or rejects a well-presented request.

- If you engage in self-advocacy as a process that relies on well-supported reasoning and keep yourself from getting upset, you will greatly increase your chances of having your request seriously considered.

Case #13

Depersonalizing Issues and Analyzing the Needs of Others

Often when you need something from an organization, you have to deal with a supervisor. This can be frustrating when the supervisor (other person) seems to have a lot on his or her mind and doesn't appear to care about what you want to say. Trying to understand what the other person is concerned about can help you reach your goals.

Nat Wants to Change His Lunch Hour at Baldwin's Hardware (revisited)

Nat has been working as a stock clerk (places items for sale on shelves) at Baldwin's Hardware store for four months. Baldwin's is open Monday through Saturday between 8:00 a.m. and 5:00 p.m. On Thursday evenings, Baldwin's has special sales and instruction on tools from 7:00 p.m. to 8:30 p.m. Nat works from 8:00 a.m. to 5:00 p.m., Tuesday through Saturday. He normally gets off for lunch from 12:30 p.m. to 1:30 p.m.

Nat's friend Harnette is getting out of the hospital on Tuesday at 2:00 p.m. Harnette needs help getting home and Nat is the only one who can help him. Nat and Harnette have plans to open their own construction company, specializing in fixing and building cabinets, shelves, and storage spaces in people's apartments.

It is 8:51 a.m. on Tuesday, the day Harnette is coming home from the hospital. Alicia is working the cash register. Danielle, the store manager, hired Alicia seven months ago. Two months ago, Alicia was given the responsibility for scheduling all the employees as well as the tool instruction events on Thursday evenings.

Before work, Alicia's mother yelled at her for staying out late. Alicia wants to go to college, but she doesn't make enough money to pay for both school and for her own apartment. Three months ago, Alicia's boyfriend died in a car accident.

There is a morning rush of customers. It is a very hot summer day. Tanya has just returned a fan because the plug fell off. She doesn't want a replacement, just her money back. Tanya is agitated and accuses Alicia of selling "junk." Three other customers are waiting in line. They are impatient and angry because Alicia hasn't let them pay for their purchases.

Alicia is uncertain whether to give Tanya her money back. She decides to lock the cash register and go find Danielle in the back of the store. Danielle never seems pleased with Alicia's decisions, and therefore, Alicia does not want to make this decision on her own.

As Alicia walks back to find Danielle, she passes Nat who is restocking light bulbs. As Alicia passes Nat, he tells her about his needs. "Hey Alicia, you lookin' down!" Alicia barely pauses as she continues toward Danielle. Nat continues as Alicia walks away. "Anyway... I'm changing my lunch hour today. I have to take my friend..."

Nat doesn't get a chance to explain that his friend is coming home from the hospital and needs his help. Before reaching Danielle, Alicia denies Nat's request. "If you change your lunch time today, don't bother coming back...ever!" As Alicia gets to Danielle's office in the back, she turns toward Nat, "You think I look down—your face scares the dead!"

Nat is furious. He has worked at Baldwin's Hardware store for four months and has never asked to switch his lunch hour. If this is the way he is going to be treated, he will quit. He will leave at 1:30 p.m. and just never come back!

Questions

1. What are the important facts that relate to the primary challenge of the case?

   a. List Nat's **long- and short-term goals.**

   b. Identify Alicia's **needs.**

   c. Identify the **needs** of Baldwin's Hardware Store.

   d. Identify Danielle's **needs.**

   e. Describe Nat's **strengths.**

   f. Identify Nat's **allies or supporters.**

   g. Identify **missing information** that would be helpful in planning strategies.

2. What must Nat do to get time off to pick up Harnette?

3. Does Alicia dislike Nat? Does it matter? Explain.

4. What are all the possible reasons that Alicia might have turned down Nat's request for a change in his lunch hour? Which of these reasons should Nat be concerned with?

5. How can Nat determine that Alicia was angry with him? Does it matter? Explain.

6. Think about why Nat got angry with Alicia and thought of quitting. How could Nat have been better prepared to keep himself from getting angry?

7. Do you think Nat was well focused on his goal? What facts lead you to think that he was not focused on his goal?

8. How could Alicia better deal with the anger of her customers?

9. In the facts of the case, it states that Harnette needs to leave the hospital at 2:00 p.m. and Nat is the only person that can pick him up. If it was *not* possible for Nat to pick up Harnette at 2:00 p.m., what other solutions could be used to get Harnette home?

10. Can you think of anyone in your life who has given you a hard time who might have similar types of pressures that Alicia is experiencing? What is the best way for you to diminish your emotional response to such an individual?

11. The case states, "Nat and Harnette have plans to open their own construction company…." Is there evidence in Nat's behavior that suggests he is in the new beginnings zone? Explain your answer.

Case #14

Connecting Your Goals with the Needs of the Organization

In evaluating whether to support your proposal, the other person will evaluate how it supports the needs and goals of his or her organization and how well suited you are to succeed if you are given the support.

James Asks Lishone for a Raise (revisited)

James has been working at Hannibal Bookstore as a clerk for two years. He is very valuable to the store because he knows how all the systems work. James also helps set up Friday night book readings and discussion groups, when authors read from their books and sign books.

Just before James's mother became very ill and he went into foster care, she told him that he should read books whenever he had time. She told him her biggest regret was not reading more. That made a big impression on James. Therefore, James really likes working in a bookstore because he loves books and it reminds him of his mother.

James makes $387 a week. His take-home pay (after taxes are taken out of his paycheck) is $324.73 a week. James has to share an apartment because rent is so high. James's monthly expenses are

Rent	415
Food	340
Telephone and utilities	49
Transportation	90
Household items	61
Medical and dental	55
Clothes	49
Personal and health items	37
Savings	50
Entertainment	85
Miscellaneous	<u>67</u>
Total	**$1,298**

(continued)

(continued)

James wants to start taking college business management classes. Someday he would like to manage a bookstore. He would even consider being a manager of one of the bookstores owned by Hannibal. Short-term, James needs to start taking college classes and needs the money to pay for them. Even at the community colleges, it will cost him $378, including books and other educational expenses, for each course.

On Tuesday, James is having coffee with Lishone Rogers, the day shift manager.

James: "Lishone, I need more money."

Lishone: "Don't we all! It seems like it goes faster than we can make it."

James: "Yeah, but I really need more money to pay all my bills."

Lishone: "Yeah, I'm going to so many clubs I can't pay my credit card."

James: "Well, should I talk to anyone about…"

Lishone: "Yeah, talk to Chase Bank. Maybe they'll give you some money. Let's get back to work."

Lishone walks away and James thinks to himself: "Damn this Hannibal Bookstore! They don't care about anyone. Screw them. This is the last time I help them with Friday's book readings."

Questions

1. What are the important facts that relate to the primary challenge of the case?

   a. List James's **long- and short-term goals.**

   b. Identify Lishone's **needs.**

   c. Describe James's **strengths.**

   d. Identify **missing information** that would be helpful in planning strategies.

2. Is it more important for Lishone to like James or to understand how James can benefit Hannibal Bookstore? Explain.

3. If you were advising James how to be a better self-advocate, how could you have prevented him from getting angry and wanting to withdraw from the Friday night book readings?

4. What are all the things Hannibal Bookstore needs from an employee to make its bookstore successful?

5. What are all the things James does or has the capacity to do that will benefit Hannibal Bookstore?

6. Using your answers from questions four and five, what are *all* the reasons why Hannibal Bookstore would benefit by paying James to take a business management class?

7. If James took business classes and remained loyal to Hannibal Bookstore, would the bookstore benefit?

8. Lishone seemed preoccupied with her own issues. She kept the conversation on a personal level. What's the best strategy to refocus the other person onto the issues you are focused on?

9. It appears likely that James is in the neutral and new beginnings zones. In order to get this far, James must have decided he is ready to end something in his life. What ending is James making in his life? What things can James do to help him through the ending you have described?

CHAPTER 7

Self-Advocacy Presentations

Background

Professional advocates, such as lawyers, make oral presentations in court or in written documents to judges and other lawyers. Lawyers also represent (advocate for) clients in different negotiations, such as signing a contract, buying a house, starting a company, settling a dispute, etc. Business professionals advocate to get customers and to gain support of their employees and the public. Political leaders advocate by making presentations to government officials, news reporters, and the general public. Employees advocate to get a job, to achieve a promotion, or to change working conditions.

As a self-advocate, you, too, will make presentations. These might be in writing, on the phone, or in a face-to-face meeting. In your presentations, you will try to persuade others to help you reach your goals and/or solve your problems.

To be a successful self-advocate, you need to use all the skills you have learned in this seminar to make a self-advocacy presentation:

- Set goals

- Make plans for how to reach your goals

- Develop a plan based on an understanding of how organizations work

- Identify personal strengths that will demonstrate likelihood of success

- Use the advice and support of mentors and allies

- Analyze the needs of the other person and depersonalize the issues

- Develop and communicate workable solutions

- Develop a compelling self-advocacy presentation through designing an effective agenda

- Use rules and laws to support you position if necessary

Agendas

Self-advocacy presentations require a written plan, called an *agenda*. It is a plan or a script for how you will make your self-advocacy presentation.

In any presentation, you need to use a written agenda to help make all the necessary points.

An agenda is your plan for making the most effective presentation. It helps you remember at the time of the presentation to include all the persuasive reasons for why the other person should support your goals. At the time of a self-advocacy presentation, it is natural to be nervous and lose the thread of your presentation. An agenda is a way to make sure you cover all your points and keep focused on your goals.

Example of Developing an Agenda

Benny has an opportunity to apply for a part-time job in the South Side Health Clinic as a health aid. Someday Benny wants to be a Physician's Assistant (PA). A PA works with a medical doctor to provide direct health services to a patient. In many cases, PAs do some medical procedures and treat minor health problems. The average salary for a PA in the year 2000 was between $48,000 and $74,000 per year. A PA needs a college degree plus two years of medical training. To plan for the interview for this part-time job, Benny researched South Side Health Clinic's services. He read their annual report, looked up newspaper articles, and used the Internet to visit their Web site and learn more about the clinic.

When Benny applied for the job, he asked and found out that the job involved assisting PAs in providing medical attention and in educating patients about health precautions they should take. This would be a great job because much of it was at night, which would enable him to continue attending college. In addition, he would learn more about health care and the work of a PA. Most importantly, he might meet people who would help him get a job after he completes college and his two years of PA training.

To prepare for his job interview (a self-advocacy presentation), Benny goes through this process:

1. Benny makes **plans** for how to reach his goals.

   Benny identifies his goals:

   a. *Complete college (he is a sophomore)*

   b. *Work part-time and summers (earn money for college and his living expenses)*

   - *Gain some practical experience in the medical field*

   - *Meet people who can help him in the medical field*

   - *Make some money to support his living expenses for the next four years in college*

   c. *In the next two years, select the best Physician's Assistant training program (usually given at medical schools)*

   d. *In two years, begin PA training*

   e. *In four years, begin work as a PA*

   To reach these goals, Benny decides that he needs to get a job at an active health care center where he can gain experience, earn money, and meet people who would help him eventually get a position as a PA.

2. Benny develops a plan based on an understanding of **how organizations work.**

   Benny knows that South Side Health Clinic provides essential medical care to a large population in the city, especially to mothers, young children, and the elderly. South Side is known for its ability to work with people from a wide range of different cultural and economic backgrounds. South Side gives excellent health care and provides essential health education to the community. South Side needs professionals who are both competent in health care skills and can relate well with people. Finally, South Side helps an underserved community, and there is often a great deal of time pressure to meet the needs of all patients. Staff must have the endurance to work under considerable stress.

3. Benny identifies **personal strengths** that will demonstrate the likelihood of success.

   Benny recognizes that his ability to work on complicated assignments in college without much supervision is a strength. He also recognizes that when he needs help, he is usually successful in getting a professor, librarian, or advanced student to help. This is a great resource for someone working in the pressure of an active health care center.

   Benny is very personable. He likes meeting new people and enjoys learning their stories. This is an excellent skill for understanding patients' health problems and gaining their trust.

   Benny also recognizes that his long-term goal of working as a PA will make him attractive to a health care clinic, because staff members will see that training Benny would benefit the clinic in the future. He may become a PA there.

4. Benny uses the advice and support of **mentors and allies.**

   Benny has become friendly with a professor who teaches a biology class. He believes this professor will write a recommendation related to how well Benny did in conducting a research assignment about the effects of high blood pressure. This directly relates to the work he would do as a PA.

5. Benny analyzes the **needs** of the other person and **depersonalizes** the issues.

   Benny realizes that he is competing with many other job applicants. He thinks that the personnel manager (the person who will do the hiring for South Side) will have a hard time deciding among so many applicants. He also realizes that the personnel manager will probably feel overwhelmed by having to interview so many people and make the final decision. Therefore, Benny doesn't expect that the personnel manager will be particularly interested or nice to him.

   Benny tries to think of ways he can help the personnel manager, and in a sense, make his or her job easier. First, he will recognize the importance of his or her job and how challenging it is to predict who will meet the needs of South Side. Benny will create a résumé that clearly states his goals, strengths, the names and relationships of allies, and his suitability for the job.

Benny knows everyone else will have a résumé. To get the personnel manager to seriously consider his application, Benny will write a cover letter. In this letter, Benny will demonstrate how he understands the needs of South Side and how his particular talents and strengths meet these needs.

Benny knows that if the personnel manager thinks he is qualified, he or she will then consider his commitment to South Side. The personnel manager will not look good if Benny only stays for several months and then leaves, or if college interferes with his work. Benny will emphasize his strong desire to succeed with this job because he is determined to develop a career as a PA. He will tell the personnel manager that he is committed to stay at the job for two to four years, until he finishes college and PA training. He also will assure him or her that as important as college is, he will make sure that he adjusts his college schedule so that it does not interfere with his work at South Side.

Benny recognizes that he cannot wait for the personnel manager to ask him these questions and must volunteer this information if he wants to be convincing.

6. Benny comes up with a **workable solution** for the personnel manager.

   Benny knows the personnel manager has a lot on his or her mind. The personnel manager may find Benny's presentation good but still not have a specific idea of how to determine whether Benny is the right person for the job. Benny knows it is up to him to come up with a reasonable solution for helping the personnel manager judge his application.

   Benny knows that many very qualified people will apply for this job. One idea Benny has is to offer to volunteer for a week to give everyone a chance to meet him and gauge his commitment and ability. This would reduce South Side's risk in making a full commitment before learning more about Benny.

This is what Benny's agenda for his job interview (self-advocacy presentation) might look like:

Benny's Agenda

1. Impressed with South Side's abilities to provide health care to so many people. (Demonstrates knowledge and respect for organization.)

   a. Particularly impressed with South Side's ability to combine good health care with compassion for the patients and their families, with emphasis on health education.

   b. To achieve their results, it must take a lot of teamwork.

   c. Would like to learn how South Side has achieved these results.

2. Have committed myself to the profession of healthcare and eventually want to work as a PA and serve people in a community health care setting. (Presents personal strengths that are important for the job.)

   a. Sophomore in college.

   b. Do well in biology and have good relationship with Professor Grobe.

   c. Grew up in D.C. housing projects and appreciate the challenges faced by people who rely on public health service.

   d. First generation to go to college, and there is nothing that is going to stop me from reaching my goal to be an excellent PA.

3. Heard you may be hiring a health aid part-time. (Presents personal goals that relate to the organization's goals.)

   a. Believe I could make a great contribution to South Side because of my interest and commitment to the field.

   b. Want to do my best because it will help me get into a good PA program.

   c. Can make a long-term commitment; any training I get will pay off for South Side.

   d. In the future would hope to work here as a PA.

   e. Can easily work night shifts because of college schedule.

4. To get to know me better, would be willing to spend a week in the clinic following around a PA and doing whatever they need. (Again demonstrates willingness to meet organization's needs and gives the organization a solution—a relatively easy way to help them make a hiring decision.)

Provide a résumé and letter stating my goals and strengths.

Self-Advocacy Presentations Require Solutions

To be a successful self-advocate, you must also have the ability to offer **solutions** for the other person. If you want help, you have to make it as easy as possible for the other person to help. Providing a solution, rather than letting the other person think of one, can save a great deal of time and demonstrate that you are well prepared.

For example, think about asking someone to write a recommendation for you. If you give that person an outline of what to focus on, and even a résumé of your accomplishments, it makes their job much easier. This provides them with a solution to the task at hand and will make them more willing to do a good job with the recommendation. Another example with a simple solution is when you need to take some time off at your job. If you make arrangements with another employee to switch times, your supervisor doesn't have to work to find someone to replace you and becomes more willing to give you that time off.

Finally, you'll notice that Ebony (from Case #2, *Ebony's First Job Interview*), who messed up her first interview with Ms. Ward, is back trying again. Ebony does not accept rejection. She believes that what she has to offer will really help E.L. Jenkins, and she tries different ways to communicate it until Ms. Ward can understand. People respect those who are not put off by making a mistake or being rejected, as long as they show they have learned how to correct their mistakes.

Concepts to Consider When Working with These Cases

- You have the responsibility for getting the other person to focus on your presentation.

- Getting the other person's focus depends on

  - Understanding his or her goals

  - Trying to support some of those goals

  - Demonstrating that support of your goals will lead to success for the other person

  - Making a compelling presentation

- A successful presentation requires you to be fully prepared. You must be completely familiar with

  - All the facts related to the presentation

  - The way you will make the presentation

  - The questions the other person is expected to ask

- Making a successful presentation requires carefully listening to and observing the other person

  - Thoughtful and difficult questions from the other person demonstrate attention and involvement in the presentation

  - Recommendations by the other person of other people to see demonstrates a faith in you

  - Attentive focus by the other person on you indicates interest in the presentation

- You must be an active listener and analyzer

  - Be prepared to take notes

  - Repeat back to the other person important information he or she has given you to make sure you understand it

  - Let the other person know how you will follow up

  - Be prepared to handle rejection of your proposal

    - Get information about **why** the other person thinks the proposal is not suitable

    - Find out if there are ways to improve the proposal

    - Demonstrate that you are not willing to give up

Case #15

Connecting Your Goals with Organizational Goals and Overcoming Rejection

You can make a perfect self-advocacy presentation and the person on the other side might still give you resistance. Learning to handle resistance and remain focused on your presentation and goals are essential skills for success. Learning how to gauge effectiveness is critical to being a successful self-advocate. Finally, a great self-advocate, such as Ebony, never accepts rejection.

Ebony's Second Interview at E.L. Jenkins

Go back and read Case #2, Ebony's First Job Interview, *to understand Ebony's situation.*

Ebony failed to get a job or internship at her first interview. She wrote Ms. Ward a thank-you note. In this note, she informed Ms. Ward that she was taking an economics class in her sophomore year at Brooklyn Community College and was thinking of majoring in business or financial management. Ebony also thanked Ms. Ward for helping her focus more clearly on her goals (this was the truth). Ebony explained that she felt in a better position to support the goals of E.L. Jenkins.

In her thank-you note, Ebony also asked if she could meet with Ms. Ward to discuss her college plans and make sure that her courses would help in pursuing a career in finance. Ebony also explained the reason she was committed to a career in finance. Ebony followed up with a phone call. While Ms. Ward was not particularly friendly, she agreed to see Ebony. Now Ebony knows what to expect.

The Interview

Ebony: "Thank you for seeing me again. I have been talking to people who work in the financial field and reading about the field, and I'm really interested."

Ms. Ward: "Yes, a lot of people think it's a road to get rich. But it is not so easy."

(continued)

(continued)

Ebony:	"Since I can remember, I have always wanted to work in a career field where I would meet many different people and be able to help them."
Ms. Ward:	"You mean as a social worker?"
Ebony:	"No...I had an uncle who was able to invest some money he made when he sold his store. Because of his investments, he was able to help his two youngest children go to college. He told me the difference between him and everyone else he knew was that he saved what little he had earned and made conservative investments in companies that had good records in making profits."
Ms. Ward:	"Sounds like good advice."
Ebony:	"Well, since then I have always wanted to learn about investing and helping others so they could afford to do things they wanted."
Ms. Ward:	"That's a good goal, but you need a lot of skills and education."
Ebony:	"I always worked hard in my math classes because I knew what I wanted to do."
Ms. Ward:	"The college you are attending is only a community college. Is that because you couldn't get into a better school?"
Ebony:	"At first I was concerned too. However, the Chair of the business department was the CEO of Hazbog Design, a marketing company with 21 million dollars of revenue (how much money they bill clients in one year). I save a lot of money by going to a community college. If my grades are B or above, which they will be, I will be able to transfer to a four-year college and major in business."
Ms. Ward:	"I see. Well, how can we help you? I already told you that at the moment we do not have any jobs or internships."
Ebony:	"I want to work in this field and want to make sure that I am doing the right things at college. I know I would be a good client representative because I make friends easily and know many people who are going to be really successful. I'm very good at explaining complicated ideas."

Ms. Ward picks up her appointment book and begins looking at her upcoming appointments.

Ms. Ward:	"Well, I wish you luck. Thanks for telling me of your plans and give me a call when you graduate."
Ebony:	"I wonder if you could ask any of the client representatives if they would like an intern. I am very good at doing research, and I know a lot of people in my neighborhood who might be interested in learning how to invest their money."

Ms. Ward: "We don't have a formal internship program."

As Ebony talks, Ms. Ward puts down her appointment book and looks at her.

Ebony: "I discussed this with my professor and he said he would be willing to supervise me if I were to do a report. I would share this report with your company."

Ms. Ward: "Sounds interesting, but I'm afraid it would be too much work, and I doubt that any client rep would be interested."

Ebony: "What if I wrote a letter explaining the purpose of my internship and my contacts in the neighborhood? Would you give it to some of the client reps?"

Ms. Ward: "Perhaps—but I would have to see the letter first before I could pass it along."

Ebony: "That would be gr..."

Ms. Ward: "Send me the letter. Don't get your hopes up. I doubt that this will work, and I think you'll be wasting your time. Perhaps you should try a bigger company that already has internships...."

Questions

1. What are the important facts that relate to the primary challenge of the case?

   a. List Ebony's **long- and short-term goals.**

   b. Identify Ms. Ward's **needs.**

   c. Describe Ebony's **strengths.**

   d. Identify Ebony's **allies or supporters.**

   e. Identify **missing information** that would be helpful in planning strategies.

2. What is the **primary challenge** to reaching Ebony's short-term goal with E.L. Jenkins?

3. Will Ebony be successful this time in getting an internship at E.L. Jenkins? Why?

4. Do you think Ms. Ward is interested in helping Ebony? What statements or actions support your observation?

5. What moments in the interview demonstrate Ms. Ward's greatest resistance to helping Ebony? Analyze what facts give Ms. Ward the greatest reason to resist providing an internship.

6. At what moment in the interview was Ms. Ward's attitude most supportive? What would be the benefits for Ms. Ward and E.L. Jenkins if Ebony were to get an internship?

7. Look at Ms. Ward's questions. Why did she ask each question?

8. How effective was Ebony in presenting her strengths?

    a. Explain how she related her strengths to the needs of E.L. Jenkins.

    b. Explain how Ebony demonstrated some of her strengths.

9. What was the value of the thank-you note that Ebony sent Ms. Ward after her first interview?

10. Ms. Ward might want to give Ebony an internship but recognizes that E.L. Jenkins has no internship program. How does Ebony help Ms. Ward solve this problem?

11. Ebony really messed up her first interview with Ms. Ward. Why was it a good idea to follow up with Ms Ward rather than just go on to another financial organization?

12. Do you think it is realistic that Ebony could have come back from such an awful interview as the one she did in Case #2, *Ebony's First Interview*? Why do you think she was able to get another interview? Think of things you have messed up and how you might have recovered. Do you think that people are more interested in how badly you messed up or your ability to recover from it? Why?

13. Was Ebony well prepared for her presentation? Explain your reasoning by giving facts and analysis.

14. For Ebony to work hard at trying to get this second interview, she probably had to make a decision to end something significant in her life. This ending was most likely tied to a particular way she viewed and responded to the world.

    a. How would you describe the ending Ebony clearly made?

b. Endings are difficult and sometimes can only be sustained temporarily. What should Ebony do to make this ending last?

Involving Your Allies

Other people familiar with your strengths and accomplishments can help you reach your goals. You have to know how to identify these people, ask them for help, and use their help.

Cheyenne's Support

Cheyenne is 17 years old. She has been in the foster care system for four-and-a-half years and has lived in three foster homes and a group home. Because Cheyenne has had to change schools so often, she is a year behind and is trying to catch up. She remembers her grandmother, whom she used to live with, saying, "Whatever happens, make sure you stick with your education."

Toshana, a friend from the group home, told Cheyenne about a self-advocacy seminar. Cheyenne followed Toshana's advice and went to the seminar, graduated, and got a certificate of self-advocacy. At graduation, the seminar teacher reminded her, "You can ask me for a letter of recommendation when you need one."

Cheyenne's only work experience was with SYEP (Summer Youth Employment Program). She worked cleaning parks. Even though the work was boring, Cheyenne completed the ten weeks without any problems and developed a good reputation with Liz Chernoff, the Director of SYEP.

Cheyenne wants to work for a bank, approving loans for families who want to purchase their first homes. She dreams of having her own home. Before he passed away, her father often said, "Cheyenne, there was one thing I wish I had done—bought my own home. I would have saved all the money I paid in rent. Listen Cheyenne, owning your own home is one of the smartest things you can do." Cheyenne wants to help others reach this dream.

To learn about banking as a career, she used the Internet and called the business departments of various colleges and mortgage lending institutions. From this information, she learned that loaning families money for homes is a very large business. The job can be very interesting because you need to understand the value of homes, types of construction, dynamics of a community, and process of financing (financing is the means of buying something like a house, a business, etc., by borrowing money). One college recommended that she major in business and eventually get a master's degree in finance or business. This graduate degree can be taken while working and is sometimes paid for by the employer.

Cheyenne read an article about a successful young man who went into the specific field of helping working people finance their first homes. This helped Cheyenne decide she wanted to try banking as a profession.

Cheyenne wrote some letters to people in the banking field. She explained her goal of wanting to help first-time buyers finance a home purchase. In the same letter, she indicated some of what she learned in her research and how she plans to pursue a degree in business/financing. Finally, Cheyenne mentioned her ability to work with different types of people. After one week, she called all seven of the people she wrote to and asked for an informational interview. One person, Ms. Jerome, Director of Residential Mortgages for First Fidelity Bank in Baltimore County, Maryland, gave her an appointment.

At the informational interview, Ms. Jerome explained what she did. Cheyenne explained how she was determined to reach her goals and how her self-advocacy training would help her set clear goals and give her the skills to help her reach these goals. Cheyenne also explained how her work at SYEP provided the experience of having a job with important responsibilities. Finally, she explained how being in the foster care system made her stronger in dealing with stressful situations and a variety of different people.

Ms. Jerome suggested that Cheyenne could try to apply for a summer internship at First Fidelity. If she didn't get an internship, she could try to get a job in the mailroom or as a messenger. Even though it would be a low-paying job, she would get to meet people who could help her and begin to get an idea about banking.

Ms. Jerome also advised Cheyenne try to work with a local nonprofit housing association that assists low-income families in finding financing for their first homes. They are often looking for volunteers, and sometimes a volunteer job can turn into a real job. Ms. Jerome suggested that Cheyenne call Gil Rodriguez who heads the coalition of affordable housing. Ms. Jerome made many other suggestions, including books and journals to read and people to contact for more information. Ms. Jerome was clearly supportive and suggested that Cheyenne keep in touch.

Questions

1. What are the important facts that relate to the primary challenge of the case?

    a. List Cheyenne's **long- and short-term goals**.

    b. Identify the bank's goals in relation to offering Cheyenne an internship.

c. Describe Cheyenne's **strengths**.

d. Identify any of Cheyenne's **allies or supporters**.

e. Identify **missing information** that would be helpful in planning strategies.

2. What is the **primary challenge** that must be resolved for Cheyenne to get a summer internship?

3. How can Cheyenne ask her allies to help her reach her goals?

4. How do you use a letter of recommendation and a reference? Which is better to have?

5. What are the values (beliefs) that Cheyenne holds? Where did she learn these values? How can they help her reach her goals?

6. Can Cheyenne reasonably consider Ms. Jerome an ally?

7. What are the advantages and disadvantages of having allies?

8. Why would any of Cheyenne's allies want to help her?

9. Cheyenne worked hard to get this very useful informational interview. She seems well on her way to making a new beginning. Most likely Cheyenne has worked her way through the endings zone and is now still in the neutral zone as well as partially in the new beginnings zone.

a. What has Cheyenne done to help herself get through the neutral zone?

b. What other things would you recommend she could do to help herself through the neutral zone?

c. Why should Cheyenne not worry about being in the neutral zone?

Case #17

Developing Workable Solutions

*When making a self-advocacy presentation, if you're lucky, you'll get to a point where the other person says, "What do you need from me?" You need to be prepared with **specific** solutions. It is not a good idea to expect the other party to come up with the specific ways to help you, even if they want to be helpful. A skilled self-advocate will develop solutions that will have minimum costs for the other person and may actually result in benefits.*

Tyshanna Needs Solutions

Tyshanna has been the night manager for 18 months at Cafémeet, a chain of small coffee cafés located in 20 major cities in the United States. She wants to keep her job but also needs more money and a more flexible schedule so she can begin college. Tyshanna's long-term future goal is to be a regional manager of a chain of stores like Cafémeet (a regional manager is responsible for a number of stores in one geographic region). Tyshanna knows that her store manager, Ms. Caldwell, respects her work.

Tyshanna's father had a hard time keeping a job after he had an accident. Her mother worked cleaning other people's apartments. Even though her mother and father had horrendous fights and never paid much attention to Tyshanna, they both told her how important it was to get a better education and do something "important with her life." At 16, to help pay for her clothing, Tyshanna worked at a daycare center for young children. Her supervisor observed that Tyshanna had a natural ability with children. She knew all the mothers and their children who come into Cafémeet. Tyshanna has also successfully encouraged her staff to pay attention to the children and make them feel comfortable while in the café.

Gloria Caldwell, Tyshanna's supervisor, has been a store manager for three years. Gloria wants to get an executive position in the central office of Cafémeet and eventually become a vice president for marketing. Gloria had a difficult start in her life. Her mother was always very ill. Her father wanted her to take care of her mother and not think about a career for herself. Gloria had to get a job when she was 16 years old. At that time her father made her give all her earnings to him in order to support her mother. As difficult as life has been, Gloria Caldwell has kept

(continued)

(continued)

focused on her goals and worked very hard. Most likely Tyshanna does not know anything about Ms. Caldwell's personal life.

On Friday at 6:43 p.m., Tyshanna, who is going on duty, bumps into Gloria Caldwell who is leaving for the weekend. "Ms. Caldwell, I've been working at Cafémeet for 18 months. I need to go to college, and I think Cafémeet should help," Tyshanna blurts out as Ms. Caldwell tries to leave the store.

As customers pass by the two of them Ms. Caldwell responds, "You know, college is a personal thing and I don't see how Cafémeet can help. Have a good weekend!" Tyshanna is furious. She thinks she's wasted 18 months, and decides to "show her," referring to Ms. Caldwell.

Questions

1. What are the important facts that relate to the primary challenge of the case?

   a. List Tyshanna's **long- and short-term goals.**

   b. Identify Ms. Caldwell's **needs.**

   c. Describe Tyshanna's **strengths.**

   d. Identify **missing information** that would be helpful in planning strategies.

2. Why wouldn't Ms. Caldwell help Tyshanna?

3. What are four problems Ms. Caldwell would have if she gave Tyshanna more flexible time?

4. How important would each of the problems you listed in question #3 be to Ms. Caldwell? Number the problems in order of their importance to her.

5. What solutions might Tyshanna suggest for all of these problems?

6. What would you include in an agenda for Tyshanna to present to Ms. Caldwell for a more flexible schedule and higher pay?

7. Tyshanna could have done a better job advocating for a raise in salary. If Tyshanna had realized that she was in the neutral zone, what could she have done that would have helped her better prepare to self-advocate?

8. Now that Tyshanna wants to be a regional manager, has she made an ending with the identification she has with her present job? Is it important? Why?

9. As in Tyshanna's case, can you make an ending with a current job position without completely leaving that company? Explain your answer.

Case #18

Developing Strategies

Individuals who are successful find many people who can help them. Finding the right people and getting them interested in helping you is hard work. Yet, it's an important step in advocating for yourself. If you identify and reach out to the right people, you can be very successful in saving time and reaching the goals you have established.

Trish Needs Informational Interviews in the Fashion World

Trish, a 17-year-old, wants to work as a fashion designer and eventually run her own design studio. She is especially interested in designing coats and jackets. To reach her goal, she wants to study both business and fashion design at college.

Trish has liked fashion since she was seven years old. Her aunt sews her own clothes and had Trish help her when she was younger. Trish always goes to see the latest fashions at all the top stores in New York City. She reads fashion magazines and sometimes reads the daily paper of the fashion world, *Women's Wear Daily*.

Trish's work experience consists of stacking books at a children's library for nine months when she was 16 years old and working as a cashier in a supermarket for the last four months.

On some occasions, Trish has had problems with her schoolwork. However, she is well liked by many of her teachers. Trish has a cousin who is studying clothing design at the Fashion Institute of Technology (FIT). FIT is a college that is part of the New York state system. Trish thinks she would like to go to FIT to study fashion design and learn something about business.

Trish had a relationship with Ricardo when she was 15 years old. Ricardo made her feel really good and capable of being successful. When Trish was 16, Ricardo disappeared. This was stressful for Trish. Since Ricardo's disappearance, she feels she has no one for support. While her parents want to be supportive, they don't make enough money and have little time left after work. For now, Trish understands that her future mostly depends on herself.

Trish has learned that a career in fashion is very competitive and few people become successful. Preparing for her career now will make it more likely she will be successful. Trish wants to learn about particular careers as a coat and jacket designer and make sure that she takes the most useful courses in college. She would also like to have a job in the fashion business while she is going to college.

Trish has done research to help her make her career plans. She found the name of a professor at FIT who is the head of the clothing design department. She also found the names of three clothing designers in New York. These people could be helpful to her.

Trish would like to have an "informational interview" with one or more of these people. An informational interview, sometimes called an informational meeting is an opportunity for someone interested in a particular profession to learn more about it from an experienced professional. At such an interview, you usually learn about the nature of the work, what education and training is necessary, some good ways of planning to enter the field, how to get internships or entry-level jobs in the field, and other ways to get more information.

The informational interview is also an opportunity to try to get the professional interested in supporting you. If the professional is impressed with your strengths and ambition, he or she might help set up other interviews for you or even help set up an internship or job interview.

Trish calls the three designers and the professor to try to set up informational interviews. She either gets a secretary or voicemail. The secretaries for the professor and one clothing designer tell her that their bosses have no available time. The other two designers never return her call after leaving a message on their voicemails.

Trish decides not to give up. She will write a letter that tries to show reasons why the professional should give her the time for an interview.

Questions

1. What are the important facts that relate to the primary challenge of the case?

   a. List Trish's **long- and short-term goals.**

   b. Identify the **needs** of the professor and the three clothing designers.

   c. Describe Trish's **strengths.**

   d. Identify **missing information** that would be helpful in planning strategies.

2. All four professionals appeared to indicate that they were too busy to talk or meet. What other reasons might they have for not responding to Trish's initial phone calls?

3. What would you include in a letter requesting an informational interview?

4. What information should Trish put in the letter that would be most appealing to the reader?

5. If Trish gets an appointment with the professor and one of the designers, what should she plan to discuss with them? Should she ask for any specific help? What help should she ask for?

6. Trish appears to have the confidence, the willingness to work, and the determination to reach her long-term goal of working in the fashion field. In moving with such determination into the new beginnings zone, Trish had to make an ending with something significant in her life. What was the likely ending Trish made?

7. Trish knows that "…her future mostly depends on herself." She is determined to get informational interviews to learn more about the fashion world, even if some people reject her requests. From these facts and others in the case, what transitional zone is Trish in? Make an argument for your selection.

Case #19

Written Presentations

Sometimes a friend or teacher may help you set up an informational interview. Other times, you have to do it yourself. For an informational interview, you need to talk with someone who has a great deal of responsibility and is usually very busy. It may be hard to set up your appointment over the phone. A letter is a good way to introduce yourself, demonstrate your seriousness, and get the person to focus on your request.

Greta Writes a Letter

Greta's future goal is to manage a hotel. Greta is 17 years old and lives with her father, two brothers, and three cousins. Her mother is no longer living, and her father has a steady job as a maintenance person and rarely is at home. Greta enjoys living in such a large family but wishes her father had more time for her and didn't have to work so much overtime.

Greta first became interested in hotel management when she went on a school trip to Washington, D.C. It was the first time she ever stayed at a hotel. She was excited with all the activity at the hotel, the different people, and the ability to make people feel good by providing a really nice room.

Greta decides that she should start preparing for her career now. She needs to know more about the different types of jobs in the "hospitality" profession, the type of education and training she will need, what classes will help her the most, and how she can get experience while she is still in high school. Greta decides she will start doing some informational interviews with high-level professionals in the hospitality field.

Greta looks up hotel management on the Internet and learns that the field is large and requires at least an undergraduate college degree. The University of Houston in Texas offers a graduate degree in Hotel Management. The next step Greta takes is to call the University of Houston. She tells the admissions officers about her interest in the hospitality field. She requests information about the school and what graduates of the program do.

(continued)

(continued)

Two weeks after her call, she receives information from the University of Houston. Greta reads all the information. She notices that one of the graduates of the Hotel Management Program is the associate manager of the Winslow Hotel in San Francisco, California.

Online Greta learns that the Winslow Hotel is a moderate-size hotel that provides individual service to its customers and specializes in small conventions and conferences. She calls the Winslow Hotel and asks for the name of the associate manager and her correct address. Jasmine Lincoln is the name she is given. She writes the following letter and decides she will follow up and call for an appointment in a week.

Greta Tubman

346 8th Street

San Francisco, California 94101

(510) 456-9864

November xx, xxxx

Ms. Jasmine Lincoln
Associate Manager
Winslow Hotel
100 Fremont Street
San Francisco, CA 94105

Dear Ms. Lincoln:

The Winslow Hotel is known for hosting successful conferences and providing excellent rooms for its customers. You must be proud of your responsibility for the hotel's success.

The University of Houston informed me that you are a graduate of the Hotel Management Program. I am interested in working in the hotel business and learning how to become a manager. I work well with different types of people and adjust very quickly to changing situations. These skills will help me in the hospitality field.

Your experience and advice would be very helpful to me in preparing for a career in the hospitality profession. I know you are extremely busy, but I would be most appreciative if you would call me at your convenience and give me a half hour of your time. Next week I will call to see if we can arrange a convenient time to talk. Thank you for your help.

Sincerely,

Greta Tubman

Greta Tubman

Questions

1. What are the important facts that relate to the primary challenge of the case?

   a. List Greta's **long- and short-term goals.**

   b. Identify Jasmine Lincoln's **needs.**

   c. How can Greta gauge the needs of Ms. Lincoln if she has never met her?

   d. Describe Greta's **strengths.**

   e. Identify **missing information** that would be helpful in planning strategies.

2. What is the **primary challenge** to reaching Greta's short-term goal of getting an appointment with Ms. Lincoln?

3. Why did Greta begin her letter by focusing on Ms. Lincoln?

4. Why doesn't Greta ask her career questions in the letter?

5. Greta's primary objective with her letter is to get an appointment with Ms. Lincoln. What are some of her other objectives in writing the letter?

6. In what ways can Greta make her letter more effective?

7. What kind of **general plan** will let Greta reach her short-term goal even if she cannot get the appointment with Ms. Lincoln?

8. What transitional zone is Greta in? Explain your opinion.

Case #20

Oral Presentations

An informational interview is a meeting with an experienced profes-
sional in a career field you have an interest in. The informational
interview is not a job interview, but rather, an opportunity to get infor-
mation about a specific job and what education, training, and experi-
ence are needed to get such a job. These types of interviews are very
important. They can help you reach your goals much faster by learning
the best ways to approach and prepare for your chosen career, and
connect you with other people who can help you achieve your goals.

People at all levels of success use informational interviews to get ahead
in their careers. Even the head of a company who is interested in
changing fields or working at a different type of company will set up
informational interviews for himself or herself in the same way as
someone who is starting out on his or her first job.

Derek Gets an Informational Interview

Derek wants to work in the video field. He is 17 years old, and although he thinks video will be a life-long career, he knows very little about the profession. Derek is completing high school next June. He has done well in a biology and history classes but not so well in many other subjects.

Derek's father was in the military, and Derek has lived in five different countries and six different cities in the United States. When Derek was 15, he was sick for six months. His parents thought he might never recover. As a result of moving so often and not being good in sports, Derek has had only a few friends in his life.

Derek has heard that many teenagers have a tough time getting started after they graduate from high school. Often they cannot find work or a suitable place to live. Many graduates from high school don't seem to ever get a job they really want. Derek has decided that he wants to have a better life. He wants to have a family someday, and he wants to work at something he will enjoy as well as make

(continued)

(continued)

a decent living. Derek thinks he would like to have a career in video. He heard that he should try to find out about what he needs to do to get into the video profession so he can be prepared.

Derek has decided to do some informational interviews. These are interviews with experienced professionals in a career field in which you are interested. The purpose of these interviews is to find out more about the field and to learn how people prepare to get jobs and begin a career in the field.

It is 7:30 a.m. on Tuesday. Derek is meeting with Sharon Simms, producer of institutional training videos. These are videos produced for companies that need to train their employees in some type of new activity.

Derek:	"Thank you for meeting with me. I understand that you started in this business as a production assistant intern and now you are producing your own shows. Your experience of starting at the bottom and then producing your own videos would be very helpful for me. I want to work in video."
Sharon:	"Have you thought about what area you would be interested in?"
Derek:	"I think I would like camera work, but I want to find out more about the entire field. Like, what's the best way to learn about the field and how do I get hired?"
Sharon:	"Why do you want to work in video?"
Derek:	"Because it looks like fun. You're not working at a desk. And everybody watches what you produce."
Sharon:	"Tell me a little about yourself."
Derek:	"I will graduate high school this June. I did very well in my biology class and in a few history classes. I enjoy reading and spend a good deal of time reading adventure novels and watching all types of programs on television. I think I'm very quick at learning how to do physical and technical things if I watch someone else do them. I've lived in many different places because my father was in the military. Although this experience was tough, I learned how to adapt to many different situations and how to deal with a lot of very different people."
Sharon:	"It sounds like you have some experiences that would be very useful. The media field is very stressful, and you have to deal with lots of different people. Learning from watching is very important."
Derek:	"Is producing video fun?"

Sharon:	"It can be fun but it's also a lot of hard work. The biggest mistake people make coming into the field is thinking it's glamorous. When you start, you spend most of the time carrying heavy equipment, getting sandwiches for the crew, and getting yelled at by producers, crew, and clients."
Derek:	"I can do that. I'm used to yelling."
Sharon:	"Then, when you make it, you spend long hours fixing problems and dealing with difficult people. The clients, the talent, and the crew can all be very difficult to deal with. Everyone is under a lot of pressure. But yes, it also can be fun when the show comes out okay, and everyone has worked hard to make it successful."
Derek:	"That must be great."
Sharon:	"You want to be a cameraperson. So do a lot of other people, so there is a lot of competition. You should also think of many of the jobs that people don't always think about. Lighting, gaffing, sound, production managing, directing, assistant producing, location scouting, researching, props, picture editing, sound editing, sound effects, music, and on and on."
Derek:	"How do I learn about what all these jobs are?"
Sharon:	"If you really want to work in this field, you can. It would be helpful to prepare in several ways. You're just at the right point to begin interning. Try to get an internship with a production company. The bigger companies usually like you to be in college before they give you an internship. But some smaller companies will take high school students."
Derek:	"How do I get an internship?"
Sharon:	"It's hard. Everyone wants them. You need to keep calling and going to as many production companies as possible. Offer your services. Tell them what you are good at. Tell them you're definitely going into the video field and you want experience and are willing to do any work to get it. Get to know as many people in the business as you can and keep pestering them, nicely of course, for an internship. You'll get one."
Derek:	"I hope so."

(continued)

(continued)

Sharon:	"And then, when you get it, treat it as a real job. Show up on time. Do the best you can. Volunteer to do more. Introduce yourself to everyone on the production. If they ask you to get lunch for everyone, don't screw up the order. If they ask you to deliver a video to an editing studio, get it there as fast as possible. Show them you are super at whatever you do. During the first years in the business, you can never think anything is beneath you."
Derek:	"Is that what you did?"
Sharon:	"I sure did."
Derek:	"What about school? Should I go to one of those video trade schools?"
Sharon:	"Maybe. But I recommend college. Look, you should talk to other people too, not just me. Get their advice. It will be different. And then you'll have to decide what advice suits you. But I'm a big believer in college. You won't get far without a college education. You have to know something about what you are videotaping, and a college education really helps. Take classes in all subjects, not just communications."
Derek:	"This has been very helpful. Are there any books I should read?"
Sharon:	"Absolutely. Read lots of novels. Videos are stories, and you need to get as much experience as possible with different ways to tell stories. Watch films. Not just new ones but old ones. Any film. Watch them again and again to see if you understand how they are made. Read some books about film and video. I'll give you a list."
Derek:	"Can you give me any suggestions of whom I might go to for an internship?"
Sharon:	"Try Meg Halpern at HYT. They are a small producer of travel videos. Also try Harold Jackson at National Express. They have their own video unit and might be interested in your experiences."
Derek:	"May I mention that you suggested I call?"
Sharon:	"Certainly."
Derek:	"Thank you so much. May I call you in a few months and let you know how I am doing?"
Sharon:	"I would like that. Sorry, I have to go now—my shoot begins at 8:00 a.m."
Derek:	"I know this is a lot to ask, but could I watch today or at some other time?"

Sharon:	"You're here. Why don't you watch this morning? I won't be able to talk with you. I'll be too busy, but you are welcome to stay."
Derek:	"Thanks, I really appreciate it!"
Sharon:	"Would you mind first getting me a cup of coffee and a muffin? I haven't had anything yet this morning. Here's some money, there is a place on the corner of 27th and Seventh."
Derek:	"Sure. I'll be right back."

Questions

1. What are the important facts that relate to the primary challenge of the case?

   a. List Derek's **long- and short-term goals.**

   b. Identify Sharon's **needs.**

   c. Describe Derek's **strengths.**

   d. Identify **missing information** that would be helpful in planning strategies.

2. What is the **primary challenge** for Derek in reaching his long-term goal?

3. What kind of **general plan** would resolve the challenge you described above and move toward Derek's long-term goal?

4. What advice does Sharon give about getting and keeping an internship? Of all the advice she gave about an internship, which would be the most helpful for you? Why?

5. Why did Derek ask to watch the morning taping?

6. What did Sharon do and say that indicates she respects Derek?

7. Why did Sharon ask Derek why he wanted to work in video? What kind of information does this give to a person in Sharon's position?

8. What are at least three important things Derek gained by doing this informational interview?

9. Derek chose to mention that he had lived in many different places. Do you think it was necessary? Why?

10. Clearly, Derek is striving to get into the new beginning zone. Yet it seems that Sharon might be suggesting that he remain in the neutral zone longer. She is really pushing college and also learning about all aspects of the video field, not just camera. Why do you think she is making this recommendation?

CHAPTER 8

Rules, Laws, and Rights

Background

Successful self-advocates know how to use rules, laws, and rights to strengthen their cases.

Television and movies make it appear as if most major disputes are solved in courts. The truth is most disputes are solved out of court. Skilled self-advocates can often resolve disputes in ways that will advance their own goals.

Example

Helen is a sophomore at Miami University. She is taking a course in basic sociology. The sociology professor suspected Helen of cheating and punished her with a lower grade. His action was unfair. Under the constitutions of the United States and Florida, the government cannot punish a person without "due process." That means that the person must be confronted by his or her accuser (her sociology professor), provided with evidence of his or her misdeed, and then given a chance to respond. This must be done in front of impartial adjudicators, usually a judge, jury, or committee of peers, who will make the final decision.

Helen first must ask whether the Constitution of the state or federal government applies (covers this case). Helen must determine whether the university is connected to the government. If it is a university run by Florida or the City of Miami and/or receives government funding, then the Constitution applies to Helen's situation and Miami University must comply with the "due process" clause of the Constitution. If the university is completely private, it does not have to comply with due process provisions of the Constitution and Helen cannot rely on the Constitution to help her get justice.

(continued)

(continued)

In Helen's case, Miami University is a state-assisted university that must comply with due process. Normally, state universities have a judicial panel made up of students and professors to resolve cases like hers. This is important, but it does not mean Helen will get quick action.

Without hiring a lawyer or using the Constitution, Helen might solve her problem more quickly and efficiently by advocating her position directly with the professor. If she does, she will not have to wait until the judiciary panel meets and she won't put the professor in a defensive position in public where he probably will be more resistant to changing her grade. If Helen first chooses to self-advocate, she still has the option of using the university's judicial panel if the professor refuses to support her position.

In the above situation, the law becomes a useful backup resource. Knowing the law gives Helen a strong self-advocacy position because she knows she has other remedies (ways of solving her problem) and can force the professor to have to submit convincing evidence if he rejects her direct appeal.

Concepts to Consider When Working on These Cases

Rules

- Most organizations have rules.

- Each organization can decide how it develops its own rules and the process in which those rules will be administered.

- These rules should be "published," meaning that they are made available to any member participant of the organization.

- The organization usually, but not always, has to abide by its own rules and, in many cases, can be forced to do so by the government.

- There are some laws (made by federal, state, or municipal government) that apply in an organization, even if they are not made by that organization.

Examples of Government Rules That Apply to All Organizations

- No organization may discriminate in hiring, firing, or promoting an employee based on religion, ethnicity, or gender.

- A person cannot be forced to reveal his or her religious beliefs.

- A public facility cannot discriminate against serving a person for racial reasons.

- A person cannot be required to do work the government believes is unsafe.

Example of a Government Rule That Does Not Apply to All Organizations

- The right to free speech does not apply within an organization. Your employer can prohibit you from speaking about certain topics that relate to work.

- Private companies do not have to comply with affirmative action hiring and promoting.

Laws

- Federal, state, and local governments make laws and regulations.

- Laws can be changed and rescinded (ended) by the same governments.

- Laws are usually followed by the majority of the citizens.

- Anyone not following a law can only be forced to do so or punished by a legal proceeding through a court. A person cannot be forced to follow a law by another citizen.

Rights

- Are a benefit or protection to engage in certain activity.

- Come mainly from government.

- Are designed to protect the less powerful and individuals who are not in the majority.

- Are not automatic—often a person must use the courts to "exercise" (protect) his or her rights.

- Are not quick ways to achieve goals or resolve problems.

Common Rights Principles

There are some general common rights principles that are at the foundation of all of our rights, laws, and most organizational rules.

Due Process

Everyone is entitled to have knowledge of the rules, laws, or rights, an opportunity to learn about any accusation against them, and an opportunity to be heard and judged in a fair and equal manner.

Equal Protection

Everyone should be treated equally regardless of age, religion, gender, race, class, etc.

Appeal Process

Usually an individual can ask someone at a higher level to hear his or her case if they disagree with the decision made.

Citizenship/Membership

In general, rules, laws, and rights apply to individuals who belong to the particular organization making these rules, laws, and rights. For example, some laws and rights only apply to citizens. The rules and regulations of Bark Motor Company cover only employees of Bark Motor Company.

Using Rules in Advocacy

Rights do not always come from laws made by the government. Rules and rights (sometimes called policies) can be made by an organization. Policies and rules can be used when you advocate for yourself in an organization. Learning how to use these policies and rules to support your objectives is an important aspect of self-advocacy.

Country Depot Gives a Warning

Ashira works at Country Depot in the paint department. Some of the rules in the Country Depot employee manual are

- Every employee must be familiar with all items sold at Country Depot and be able to guide a customer to the location of any given item.

- To maintain a professional atmosphere and encourage customer requests, employees must keep any socializing with other employees to a minimum.

Ashira has worked at Country Depot for five weeks. She works in the paint department as a junior associate. Prior to working at Country Depot, Ashira painted apartments for J&J Painting Company. Since she was a teenager, Ashira decided that an important long-term goal would be to get a good job that would allow her to advance to higher positions if she worked hard. She also wanted a job that would give her and her family medical benefits and pension benefits so she could afford to have a family. She likes Country Depot and would someday like to manage a department, a shift, and eventually, an entire store.

Ms. Hale is Ashira's supervisor. Ms. Hale was transferred from another Country Depot store that was closer to her home. She is particularly hard on new employees and doesn't appear to give them the benefit of the doubt. Ashira has already had two minor run-ins with Ms. Hale and tries her best to stay out of her way.

Ms. Falcon is the store manager. She is well regarded by the Country Depot organization because customers respect her particular store for its good service. She receives the fewest customer complaints and she has the longest tenure (time someone stays at a job) of employees in all the Country Depot stores in the region.

(continued)

(continued)

On Wednesday, a customer asked Ashira where she could find romex connectors. Ashira had no idea what a romex connector was. The customer told her it's an electrical part. Ashira walked the customer to the electrical area. She found Latoya, another Country Depot employee, and asked her to help the customer.

After Latoya finished with the customer, Ashira asked Latoya if she could teach her more about electrical supplies. Latoya explained how she learned about electrical supplies and the kind of work she did before joining Country Depot. Latoya has worked at Country Depot for 19 months and has the rank of senior associate. Her stories helped Ashira understand more about the different components needed for electrical work.

Ashira's supervisor, Ms. Hale, passed by the aisle where Ashira and Latoya were talking. Ms. Hale paused about 25 feet away and noticed Ashira out of her department and intensely engaged in conversation with Latoya.

On Thursday, Ashira received a red warning notice. This notice stated that she was observed socializing away from her station during her working hours. Ashira was notified that a disciplinary notice would be placed in her personnel file. Any such notice will put off promotion for at least nine months.

Ashira believes that she has been unfairly accused and punished. She wants to remain at Country Depot and reach her long-term goals. If she allows this notice to be placed in her personnel file, she will be prevented from moving ahead with her goals.

Questions

1. What are the important facts that relate to the primary challenge of the case?

   a. List Ashira's **long- and short-term goals.**

   b. Who at Country Depot is in a position to help Ashira?

   c. Identify the **needs** of the person in a position to help Ashira.

   d. Describe Ashira's **strengths.**

   e. Identify Ashira's **allies or supporters.**

   f. Identify any **missing information** that would be helpful in planning strategies.

2. What is the **primary challenge** that must be resolved for Ashira to reach her short- and long-term goals?

3. What rules would help Ashira have the disciplinary notification rescinded (taken back, canceled)?

4. What are all the facts Ashira should consider in building her case to have the disciplinary letter rescinded?

5. What are other examples of rules that are established in private organizations?

6. How can Ashira resolve this challenge without putting herself in a more difficult position with Ms. Hale?

7. What personal reason might Ms. Hale have for punishing Ashira? Does it matter in planning a self-advocacy strategy?

8. Ashira appears ready to use self-advocacy to keep her position at Country Depot. This is an important decision because she could just quit or let the warning go without any response. What are the advantages and disadvantages for Ashira in making a self-advocacy presentation to Ms. Falcon?

9. Does Ashira's determination to keep her position indicate that she is in any specific transition zone? Does her action suggest that she has made an ending with part of her past life? Explain your answers.

Case #22

Applying Rules, Laws, and Rights in Self-Advocacy Presentations

Knowledge of the law can be useful in self-advocacy. Laws can be thought of as agreed upon rules that will be respected for resolving disputes. In most cases, knowing the laws and using your understanding of the laws will help to resolve a dispute without having to go to court.

Example of Laws Supporting Jill

- There are state laws that protect consumers when they purchase a new product. Such laws provide that a new product is expected to work as designed even if there is no written guarantee.

- There are also laws that require merchants to fairly represent (accurately describe) what they sell.

- In many cities, there are laws that require landlords to paint apartments for new tenants and to keep the appliances in working order.

- Knowing these laws make most merchants (people who sell things), landlords, customers, and tenants capable of resolving problems without going to court.

Jill Battles Back

Jill has been saving money since she was 17 years old so she could go to college to study environmental science. Jill wants to work to protect the environment for future generations of children. She believes that many environmental dangers are invisible; therefore, the community needs scientists who will detect the dangers and protect the public from them.

When Jill was 18, she realized she wanted to move away from her parents. This meant she would have to pay all of her expenses.

Jill is now 20 and beginning her third year at Lone Star City College in Houston, Texas. The decision to leave home was a very difficult one, but she felt she was ready and wanted a change. She just left home and is setting up her apartment. Last week she signed a lease for an apartment for $589 per month. It is a small apartment. The landlord said he would paint the apartment and fix the stove, which does not work. When Jill signed the lease, she gave the landlord $1,178—one month's rent and a security deposit.

Jill's apartment came totally unfurnished. Nothing was in the apartment except the kitchen appliances. Jill purchased a new television set at Best Deal Appliances for $219. She also purchased a secondhand bed and bureau at Harper's Slightly Used furniture store. The salesperson told Jill that the bed was only a couple of years old and that the bureau was built in 1911 when "things were really built well. It's an antique!" Jill paid $85 for the bed and $218 for the bureau because it looks so nice and she likes old things.

Jill has been a great student. She has worked very hard, and some of her teachers think she can get a scholarship to graduate school. In graduate school, she will get her master's degree in environmental science and then be in a position to work for companies that specialize in reducing carbon pollution. This is great news for Jill.

Unfortunately, while Jill has devoted so much time to her college work, she encountered some problems in setting up her apartment. The landlord has only painted her bathroom and has not fixed the stove. The TV she purchased was delivered in an opened box, the set was obviously scratched, and the sound volume was erratic. The bed she purchased was missing a leg and when she put clothes in the bureau, the drawers collapsed. The bureau was put together with tiny staples and lots of thin plastic.

Last Thursday, Jill opened her mail and found a credit card statement in her name and address for $1,723. She never opened this credit card account. Someone had obviously taken her information and fraudulently opened the account. She is worried that if she doesn't correct the problem, she will have a bad credit rating and she will never be able to get a legitimate credit card or loan.

Questions

1. What are the important facts that relate to the primary challenge of the case?

    a. List Jill's **long- and short-term goals.**

    b. Identify the **needs** of the appliance store, used furniture store, and the landlord.

    c. Describe Jill's **strengths.**

    d. What facts are important for Jill to collect in resolving her various problems?

    e. Identify any **missing information** that would be helpful in planning strategies.

2. What is the **primary challenge** that must be resolved in order for Jill to resolve the problems that she had encountered in setting up her apartment?

3. Often individuals in Jill's situation can resolve most of these problems with direct communication—by calling the merchant, landlord, and credit card company. In all of the situations presented in this case, the law is most likely on Jill's side. Even so, there will be times when this will not be sufficient. Assume that Jill meets with initial resistance when she makes the first calls to solve her problems. What kind of self-advocacy strategy would work for

    a. Exchanging the television?

    b. Repairing and painting the apartment?

    c. Getting a refund for the bureau and bed?

    d. Resolving the incorrect credit card charge?

4. Why are laws and courts needed if most problems, where civil laws (transactions between individuals, **not** crimes) have been violated, are resolved outside of the court system?

What Is an Informational Interview?

Getting and conducting an **informational interview** is an essential element in planning a good career strategy. In all fields and areas of interest, there are people who have developed a great deal of experience and knowledge. These "experts" have experience and knowledge that can be extremely helpful to you for **learning what you need to do** to reach your career goals and making contacts for an internship or additional informational interviews.

Informational interviews have other benefits: a referral (introduction, recommendation) to other prominent experts, a referral or opportunity to get an internship, special consideration for acceptance into a college, a possible future reference, etc. Many people refer to these additional benefits as **networking**. Networking is a way to make contacts with influential people who can be helpful to you in pursuing your goals.

You may feel that an informational interview is all one-sided. The other person is just doing you a favor. In fact, it is a bit one-sided in that you are just beginning to think about a career and the person with whom you are meeting has many years of experience in the field. Therefore, it is up to you to make the other person see value in what he or she is doing for you in this meeting. This requires a great self-advocacy presentation that includes

- Fully understanding your goal and what specific information you want

- Making the expert (other person) feel you are going to be a success

- Demonstrating that you value the information and advice you receive

Point to remember:

- The clearer you are in communicating your goals, the easier it is for the other person to help you.

- Your ability to present your strengths will increase the expert's interest in helping you get specific information and assistance.

- You will increase the motivation of the expert to help you if you can demonstrate that you value his or her information and advice.

- If you follow up by communicating to the informational interviewer your progress in pursuing their advice, it will keep them interested in you and thinking of you when new opportunities arise.

- All successful people engage in informational interviews throughout their lives.

Method and Example of Briefing a Case

When you are assigned a case, 1) read it through to get an overall understanding of the story; 2) review all the questions you must answer to brief the case; 3) re-read the entire case to discover your answers for each question. On your second reading of the case, it might help if you mark up (write in the margins of) the case.

Suggestions:

- While reading the story a second time,

    - <u>Underline</u> important facts.

    - Write **G** in the margin next to the main character's **goals.**

    - Write **N** in the margin next to **needs** of the other people in the case.

  - Write **S** in the margin next to **strengths** of the main character (the person who the case is about).

  - Write **P/C** in the margin next to **primary challenge** the main character faces.

For most cases, you have to answer the following questions:

1. What are the important facts that relate to the primary challenge of the case?

    a. List the main character's **long- and short-term goals.**

    b. Identify the **needs** of the person in a position to help the main character.

    c. Describe the **strengths** of the main character.

     d. Identify **missing information** that would be helpful in planning strategies.

2. What is the **primary challenge** that must be resolved (worked out) for the main character to reach his or her long- or short-term goals?

3. What kind of **general plan** would resolve (work out) the challenge you described above and move toward the main character's long-term goal?

Example of Briefing a Case

The following is an example of how Case #2, "Ebony's First Job Interview," could be briefed. This is a model of a well-briefed response to the first three questions. It may take you several exercises before you can make the necessary analysis to brief a case this thoroughly.

1a. List the main character's (Ebony) long- and short-term goals.

Long-term:

- Protect her future children

- Find an interesting career with a good income

- Take control of her life

- Choose a career within the business field

Short-term:

- Get a better job than working at King Burger

- Learn more about business

- Help her father pay rent next year

- Develop good job contacts for when she graduates in two years

- Complete college

- Get a job to learn more about possible careers and to make money for additional living expenses

- Reverse the bad interview she had at E.L. Jenkins

1b. Identify the goals of the person in a position to help Ebony, the main character.

Ms. Ward works in personnel. Her job is to find talented and skilled employees who will benefit E.L. Jenkins. Ms. Ward's own reputation depends on the performance of the people she hires as well as how long they stay at E.L. Jenkins. Before Ms. Ward will hire anyone, she needs to have enough solid information to feel confident that the individual she hires will work well, will be committed to the investing field, and will develop loyalty to E.L. Jenkins.

Because a mutual fund company must have many customers, the company needs employees who are good at communicating with customers and at explaining the company's services. E.L. Jenkins invests other people's money, so they must hire employees who are responsible and serious. The company also needs someone who is good at understanding numbers. Employees must have this skill for actual investing as well as explaining the value of E.L. Jenkins to its customers.

1c. Describe the strengths of Ebony.

- Good student

- Strong in math

- Stays with a challenge for a long period

  - Received a high school diploma

  - Is a sophomore at college

  - Maintained receptionist job for the entire summer

- Strong motivation to succeed

  - Have a family

  - Protect her children

  - Work in an important career

- Sense of pride
  - Dresses well despite not having much money
  - Overcame challenges in high school to graduate and go on to college
  - Wants to find out more about opportunities in the field of business
- Ability to overcome adversity, deal with difficult situations, and adapt to change. Also has practice in changing her life patterns.
  - Experience as a receptionist
    - Handles professional responsibility
    - Successfully identifies with an organization's needs
    - Makes people feel comfortable

1d. Identify any missing information that would be helpful in planning strategies.

In analyzing the interview, Ebony needs to

- Have more specific ideas of what she would like to do at E.L. Jenkins to answer Ms. Ward's question, "What department would you like to work in?"
- Give more specifics in explaining her long-term goals to answer the question "What are your plans for the future?"
- Learn more about E.L. Jenkins

2. Describe the primary challenge to reaching the long- and short-term goals of the central character.

Finding a way for Ebony to reverse the negative effects of her interview with Ms. Ward and receive another opportunity to get an internship.

3. General plan

- Find out more about type of work and responsibilities at a mutual fund company

- Through a thank-you note to Ms. Ward, Ebony should
  - Make a strong presentation to Ms. Ward about Ebony's strengths
  - Demonstrate more knowledge about E.L. Jenkins
  - Show how Ebony's strengths would be of value to E.L. Jenkins
  - Display a desire and ability to commit to supporting the goals of E.L. Jenkins
  - Communicate a strong desire to work at E.L. Jenkins by explaining some of Ebony's future goals as well as offering to learn more about the company through an internship

Guidelines for Writing a Self-Advocacy Letter

Writing a self-advocacy letter requires a combination of self-advocacy strategy and creativity. Whether you consider yourself a good or poor writer, you need to look at this project as a communication process:

- What is the most effective way to communicate with the other person?

- How do I get his or her attention and interest?

- How do I get this person to believe in me?

- How do I get this person to recognize my seriousness and ability to succeed in my goals?

The following is a *suggested* outline. Your style of communication or the situation may call for many other ways to write a self-advocacy letter.

First Paragraph: Areas That Interest the Reader to Get His or Her Attention

Your first paragraph must **get the reader's attention**. Start by focusing on the reader, *not* on yourself.

Begin with a statement that explains what you see as the purpose of the organization that this person represents:

- "Country Depot is known for having salespeople who know where merchandise is located and know how to use home-building materials."

- "Your work as an engineer has such importance for constructing efficient and usable buildings."

- "The Brahmin Agency is known for helping youth develop successful working careers."

Do **not** focus on your goal/problem/issue in this first paragraph!

Second Paragraph: Strong Statement About Who You Are

Your reader wants to work with and help others who are successful. You must present yourself as a talented, mature, and persistent individual. Convey the idea that you are going to be successful with your life and that if the organization is associated with you, it will look successful too!

Third Paragraph: Your Goal

Present your goal in the most powerful manner. Include all the **benefits** for the reader and his or her organization if you achieve this objective. Be as dramatic as possible.

Fourth Paragraph: Connect Your Objective to the Goals of the Organization

(**Note:** You may need more than one paragraph.)

Try to connect your goal with the ability to benefit the organization.

- If your goal is to get a salary increase or financial support to take a class and improve your accounting abilities, you might write

  I would like to meet with you to discuss ways I could be of more help on the financial side of the bakery.

- If your goal is to get an informational interview to learn about bread baking as a career, you might write

  Your particular experiences as a bread baker would be so important in helping me learn how to become a professional baker. If you could give me 30 minutes of time at your convenience, I would be most appreciative.

- If your goal is to change your work days but work longer hours, you might write

  I would like to meet with you to discuss ways I could give C&E more work hours.

- If your goal is to be moved from your present job into sales, you might write

  I would like to meet with you to talk about ways I could be more helpful to customers.

Try to make the solution seem simple and easy to achieve. You want the decision-maker to believe that the cost of helping you is very little compared with the benefits. That is why benefits must always be heavily emphasized and problems de-emphasized.

Fifth Paragraph: Follow-Up Action

The purpose of your letter is to get the reader **interested** in helping you. Ideally, you want your needs to be met, but unfortunately, that does not usually happen right away. In most instances, it is useful to ask for a meeting with the person in authority so you can make a complete presentation.

The reader of your letter (a decision-maker) usually is very busy and focused on issues other than yours. There is little reason for them to take action if they can avoid it. Don't assume you will get a response. Instead, tell the reader you will take the next step. This reminds the decision-maker that you will not disappear. The next action does not have to be big. You can just call to make an appointment, call to answer questions, or suggest that you will have a person on "your side" call her or him.

SAMPLE LETTER for Requesting an Informational Interview

Cheyenne Steadfast
23 West 267 Street
New York, NY 10111
212-444-7896

February xx, xxxx

Ms. Jody Kole, Vice President Residential Mortgages
BK Mortgage Associates
22 Queens Boulevard
Queens, New York 10999

Dear Ms. Kole:

BK Mortgage Associates is known for helping first-time home buyers get a mortgage. Your reputation for helping many first-time home buyers has attracted many hard-working families to your services. Ms. Jaspor, a mortgage broker at your Sunnyside branch office, suggested that you would be a good person to contact.

Next September I plan to begin college. I will major in business and am interested in a career in finance, specifically as a mortgage lender. I have worked at a number of jobs to help save money for college. Through this experience, I have learned that budgeting for expenses is an extremely important skill. Assisting others to develop this skill can be very important for helping families afford their own houses.

My goal is to learn about the banking and mortgage profession and complete a college education. In the future, I would like to work as a mortgage officer at a mortgage brokerage or bank.

Your advice and experience in helping me plan my career in banking and plan ways that I might someday be useful to BK Mortgage Associates would be appreciated. I will call next week to see if I can schedule a 30-minute appointment at your convenience.

Sincerely,

Cheyenne Steadfast

Cheyenne Steadfast

Presentation Agendas

To make a convincing self-advocacy presentation, you need an **agenda**. An agenda is a **plan** for making a presentation. Think of it as a script. It tells you what to do throughout your presentation.

An agenda helps you make sure that you cover all the important parts of your presentation. Every successful presentation, whether for a job, a promotion, a court case, a business contract, a good lease from a landlord, specific help from a teacher, etc. will benefit from using an agenda. Most people put their agendas into written notes and use them at their meetings. Some people use notes printed on paper and others find using index cards easier to manage.

The Setting for the Meeting

In preparing for any meeting, you need to **know as much about the person you are presenting to as possible**. If you have no information, assume the following:

- The person has many responsibilities and pressures associated with his or her job.

- The person is **not** interested in you. This is not personal; it is because this person is most likely focused on his or her own job responsibilities.

- The person is usually very busy and has no time for new ideas or projects unless they clearly advance the goals of the organization or meet some particular need.

- You will usually be interrupting the person's normal job routine, and he or she will still be focused on something related to his or her job rather than you.

You need to find a way to get the other person to focus on you. This usually involves focusing on the needs of his or her organization, making a presentation that attracts attention, and meeting the personal needs of the other person.

Model Agenda

A good self-advocacy agenda has a specific order in which you will deliver information and persuasive reasoning. You usually begins the self-advocacy presentation by getting the attention of the other person, finding out about the needs of the other person, and presenting convincing facts that demonstrate how supporting you will also advance the goals of the other person.

During any presentation, there is a tendency to become nervous or distracted by the questions and information presented by the other person. Having a written agenda, a plan, will help you remember to cover all the important material.

1. **Develop a connection with the person in authority**

   Regardless of whether you like someone, you can respect one or more of his or her following characteristics:

   - Expertise and knowledge

   - Professional accomplishments, and, thus, his or her advice

   - Position of responsibility in the organization

   - Some specific characteristics you have learned about the person

   By communicating your respect, you acknowledge that the person is in a key position to help you. This is important for two reasons:

   - It makes the person feel good about this particular meeting because you are relating to something he or she is knowledgeable about and has a passion for.

   - It may be hard to believe, but at the beginning of your presentation, the other person is nervous too. The person is not sure what you will want and whether he or she has the ability to do what you need. If you first relate to the individual's areas of expertise, you reduce his or her nervousness.

2. **Communicate the reason why the person might want to help you**

Give the person feedback that you understand the objectives/needs of the individual's organization as well as his or her own personal objectives. Helping you reach your goals may advance those goals. Remember, this person has a great deal of responsibilities and pressure, and he or she needs to have a good reason to help you.

3. ***Briefly* get the person interested in the *positive* part of you**

You may start by telling the other person your goals/objectives. Remember to let the individual know you are going to be successful. Next, you may talk a bit about your strengths, particularly if they relate to the objective of your presentation. Try to relate this to the objectives of your meeting.

4. **Explain the purpose of your meeting**

   - Your objective

   - How it can **support the needs of the individual's organization**

   - **Specifically what the person can do for you** (this is the heart of your presentation)

   - Other suggestions the individual might make to help you achieve your objective

5. **Prepare to answer questions the individual might have for you**

You need to prepare for questions the individual might have for you. If you are interviewing for a job, you should be prepared with information that would support why you would be good for the job, how you have acquired knowledge of the field, etc.

6. **Closing: Express appreciation for time and help offered and mention next steps**

   - Thank the individual for his or her specific help

   - Repeat whatever advice was offered by the individual

   - Explain how you will follow up

Sample Agenda

Cheyenne has made an appointment to meet with Ms. Davis, the head of the loan department at BK Mortgage Associates. Ms. Davis's secretary made it clear that she would only have 15 minutes available. Cheyenne's objective is to **get a job** in finance/lending to learn more about mortgage lending and to support herself when she goes to college.

Note: As with any planned agenda, the other person, in this case Ms. Davis, may interrupt and change the order and nature of the presentation. The agenda will help Cheyenne get back to her objectives if she is interrupted and not forget the most important parts of her presentation.

1. **Develop a connection with the person in authority**

   1. I appreciate Ms. Davis meeting with me

   - Ms. Davis's extensive experience in banking and mortgage lending is extremely important to me

   - Appreciate taking time to help me

   - Recognize importance of her position as head of residential mortgage lending:

     - Insures good loans for bank

     - Helps individuals in community purchase homes

2. **Communicate the reason why the person might want to help you**

   2. I understand BK's importance in community

   - BK has a reputation for helping first-time homebuyers gets loans to purchase homes

   - Career goal is to work in mortgage field

     - Dedicated to becoming a top mortgage broker by learning everything about field and working hard with my clients

   - Want to learn and contribute to BK

3. **Briefly get the person interested in the positive part of you**

    3. Interested in banking and particularly loan work for many years

    -   Want to make a career in loan work—will study business and finance at college

    -   Recognize that mortgage brokers can increase base of customers who responsibly pay off their loans if they can educate clients about how to handle budgeting and project their monthly expenses

    -   Because of keen interest in learning about lending, would be eager to learn any job in the loan department

4. **Explain the purpose of your meeting**

    4. Need advice on how to develop a career in mortgage lending and how to begin working at an institute like BK

    -   Would like to find a job that would put me in a position to begin learning more about loan work and help pay my expenses for college

    -   Believe that my commitment to learning about the field would help a loan department because

        -   If I was eventually hired by BK, I would know specifically about their services

        -   Using over a longer period of time the training and knowledge I learned since I would want to stay at the job

        -   I would learn faster because of my motivation

        -   It could reduce costs to BK by training me while I'm an intern

    -   Can Ms. Davis let me know when an entry-level job comes up in the loan department?

    -   Can Ms. Davis suggest the best way to go about getting such a job?

    -   Does Ms. Davis have any other ideas about what I should do to develop a career in bank lending?

5. **Prepare to answer questions the individual might have for you**

   5. Information that supports my abilities

   - Names and phone numbers of references

   - Certificates, awards, letters of recommendation, etc.

   - Résumé of any working and skills experience, plus ways to reach me

   - Could work from 9:00 a.m. to 5:00 p.m. and would take college classes at night

   - Have good record in math classes

   - Worked as an assistant to the cook in a group home last summer; was a tedious job, yet stayed with it the entire summer and have good reference from the cook

6. **Closing: Express appreciation for time and help offered and mention next steps**

   6. Thanks for your time and especially your advice

   - Will use your advice to pursue my career goals.

   - Can I call you in a few weeks to see if any jobs become available?

   - May I call you to follow up on your advice?

Sample Thank-You Letter to an Informational Interviewer

Letter must be on good paper and preferably printed off a computer. No spelling or grammatical errors!

Your name
Your address
Your phone number
Your e-mail address

Date

Name
Title
Company name
Address

Dear Ms./Mr. Last Name:

It was a pleasure meeting with you last Tuesday. I appreciate the advice you gave me about_____. *(indicate two or more valuable pieces of information you gained from the interview.)*

Your expertise and experience is of great value. After meeting with you, I have a better idea of how to plan my future. Your suggestion that I_____ *(give one or more specific steps the person recommended for you to take to reach your goals)* _____ _____ is a good one.

Thank you for all the time you spent with me and sharing your experiences and advice. I'll keep you informed of my progress in pursuing my career in_____.

Sincerely,

Your signature

Your full name